ELECTRONIC CONTACT WITH THE DEAD

What Do the Voices Tell Us?

ELECTRONIC CONTACT WITH THE DEAD

What Do the Voices Tell Us?

BY

ANABELA CARDOSO

www.whitecrowbooks.com

Praise for
Electronic Contact With the Dead

This is the second book by Anabela Cardoso about unusual experiences revolving around voices from other dimensions. As with her previous book *Electronic Voices*, the author continues to explore the Instrumental TransCommunication (ITC) phenomenon, which claims to investigate contact with the deceased.

To some, including the author, these communications support the hypothesis of survival of consciousness after bodily death. Most of these communicators identified themselves as deceased humans and they usually communicated through radio speakers and/or on recorded magnetic tape with the experimenter. Sometimes they carry on lengthy dialog regarding various topics including descriptions of their world, as well as spiritual teachings regarding the purpose of life.

Many of these scenarios are quite different from religious teachings and commonly held Western assumptions about the experience of bodily death. At the same time, the author claims to have received telepathically messages, but gives the disclaimer, "The information I receive telepathically is not always right." This is a book that needs to be read with an open mind and a critical perspective. Even so, it is extremely well written, so much so that I found the book hard to put down once I had started it.

~ Stanley Krippner, Ph.D., Co-editor, *Varieties of Anomalous Experience: Examining the Scientific Evidence*

Anabela Cardoso's book is a unique achievement, of inestimable importance for our life—and I use the term "life" in the broad context in which it means not only this biological life but our continuing existence in the universe. Because we are not confined to this life alone: we live in this dimension and live also in another - perhaps many others. Anabela's communicators make this clear. It's strange that not all people are deliriously happy to receive this message, but instead some doubt its veracity. What do we need to understand who we really are? Not just flesh-and-bone organisms, but continuously existing beings in an information-based, harmoniously structured universe?

It would be in our best interest to accept the possibility that we can communicate with those who have already passed into another dimension, because we will all pass into that dimension, and what we do here and now will no doubt have an effect on our passing there and then.

The great, nearly unique virtue of Anabela Cardoso's book is that it tells us who we really are. Tells us clearly, without bias - tells us the way it is. Because Anabela knows the way it really is: she has heard it with her own ears. She has no doubt about it, nor will we doubt it once we read her book with the clear, honest, and open mindset with which she wrote it.

Few gifts can equal the gift this book offers to immortal beings who entertain the illusion that they are mortal. I am happy to receive this gift from her—and so will every reader who is open enough to receive its message. This is the fruit of a lifetime devoted to a clear-headed investigation into a most amazing reality, which turns out is the reality we have known through the ages and had almost forgotten. With books such as this, we can recover.

~ ERVIN LASZLO, P.H.D., AUTHOR OF *WHAT IS REALITY?: THE NEW MAP OF COSMOS, CONSCIOUSNESS, AND EXISTENCE*

CONTENTS

INTRODUCTION

Instrumental Transcommunication (ITC) is a novel method of attempting contact with another dimension where, as our communicators tell us, the deceased live. The contact is accomplished through electronic devices and this is the main difference compared to methods of the past. Besides, in ITC, the contact between the experimenter on the earth and communicators in another dimension happens without intermediaries. And this is the new method's major achievement. Indeed, direct contact with us here on the earth was the communicators' chief priority when scientists in the next world finally developed the new electronic way, as Timestream communicators informed the ITC operators in Luxembourg, Maggy and Jules Harsch-Fischbach (Locher and Harsch, 1989).

The electronic voices received through ITC tell us that they originate "in another dimension beyond time, a world where the dead also live". My own contacts have been with voices that, overall, assert that they belong to the deceased; hence the title of this book. Naturally, this does not mean that only the dead from our world live in the dimension that I, and other ITC operators, have contact with. Beings from other origins live there also, as Timestream communicators stated in Luxembourg years ago. But in my case, the voices have repeated time and again that they "are the dead speaking from another world".

So far, it has not been proven that these voices are produced normally. Consequently, we should seriously investigate and enquire: do the dead speak to us from another world? Of course the question is similar to: do the dead survive death? Taking into consideration the exemplary reception conditions of many of the communications we will be discussing, I firmly believe scientists should have taken this basic step long ago. However, they did not. Instead, they have avoided the subject by ignoring it, thus trying – and in most cases succeeding – to discredit it and make it fall into oblivion.

Yet, serious claims in the field of anomalous electronic contacts cannot easily be discarded. The anomalous voices exist beyond any doubt; some of them speak loudly, clearly and coherently; the content of what they say can be understood by any normal person who is not deaf and knows the language they are using.

Most of the time the voices affirm that they are the dead, reply to questions and identify themselves with names; sometimes they also ask questions and, frequently, make statements. But let me clarify that, when I speak of the electronic voices, it should be understood, implicitly, that I mean good, genuine, intelligible voices that can easily be identified. Sadly, all of us in this field know that many claims of recorded electronic voices (and images) are not trustworthy. However, because some of the proclaimed voices are just the result of pure pareidolia – i.e., the result of wishful thinking or projection of meaning onto random blurred noise – or even plain fraud, that cannot dismiss the fact that many electronic communications are entirely genuine.

Obviously, when I make assumptions and, sometimes, reach conclusions about the electronic communications, I am referring only to the real ones as described above. I disregard entirely the multitude of blurred, wrongly interpreted, or even false electronic voices publicly presented as anomalous communications, particularly through the Internet.

I beg my readers to keep this statement in mind and I take the opportunity to appeal to their critical sense at the time of examining whatever is presented to them as "electronic communication with the dead". They should, unremittingly, do it under the light of judicious and thorough judgment. This is indeed a most important condition that cannot be over-emphasized. Anyone interested in exploring this fascinating area of study and research should keep it in mind at all times.

I believe that, in its essence, life consists more of probabilities than of certainties. Once realized, probabilities appear to us as certainties but in reality they are not. A certainty is just a probability that came true. As we will see, the anomalous voices are a clear example of this assumption.

I also think that nothing is one-sided, not even double-sided; everything is multi-sided in our world and, particularly, in such an elusive area of research as our field of interest. Furthermore, we cannot grasp all the facets of anything, even of the simplest of things. We think we can, of course, but in reality we cannot.

Hence, if I manage to help unveil a new facet of this fascinating field, or even clarify some of the topics previously discussed by me and other researchers, I will have accomplished my main purpose in life: that is, to contribute to the serious study and systematic investigation of the extraordinary electronic voice-phenomenon.

Those mysterious voices that come from 'nowhere' and tell us "We are the dead speaking from another dimension beyond time" (Cardoso, 2010) have not yet been understood and explained even less. But they need to be. I believe this goal is vital for humanity and our world as a whole.

My own experimentation and research has been mostly with audio ITC. The voices convey information and I consider that to be of the utmost importance, so this is indeed my preferred area of exploration.

In this book I will deal also with 'telepathic impressions', i.e. information I perceive mentally, either spontaneously or in reply to my mental questions, which seem to be inspired by my ITC communicators. Other experimenters have reported similar occurrences since, and as early as, Friedrich Jürgenson's time, by the middle of the 20th century. It seems that ITC and very likely other methods of endeavouring to contact the invisible side of life may open the doors of perception in some unknown way.

I will quote and paraphrase ITC messages received from my, and others', communicators but those will clearly be indicated so that the reader can differentiate exactly between the information that comes from my mind and sensitivity (inspired or not by my communicators) and the objective, recorded information I, and others, received and registered in the form of electronic voices apparently originating in another dimension.

Whenever the occasion arises, I will also compare messages of similar content received in far-away points of the globe by ITC operators who did not know each other or each other's work.

In this book I will reveal to my readers subtle and often subjective aspects of the situations experienced by me as an ITC operator, or related to the environment, or both, which, hypothetically, may be relevant to the reception of the anomalous electronic voices. Naturally, some of the latter, by their very nature, cannot be verified. But I will indicate what was perceived subjectively by me and what was conveyed loudly and clearly by my communicators from Rio do Tempo Station through their verbal communications. The latter will be between inverted commas.

Readers must be prepared to take in information that contradicts our current values and the understanding most of us have of life, which greatly challenges the current paradigm. In many instances it totally reverses it. But breaking with the established paradigm seems to be one of the main purposes of ITC as we will see later in the book.

I will focus mainly on the objective information received from our communicators but will also deal with subjective experiences and impressions. From these I will draw personal reflections and, perhaps, conclusions. Above all, I will endeavour to open further the path to the exploration and understanding of the anomalous electronic voice-phenomenon.

Chapter 1

A Brief Presentation of
Instrumental
Transcommunication (ITC)

S ince the time of the great pioneers and heralds of the electronic
voices, Friedrich Jürgenson and Dr Konstantin Raudive, many
works have been published on the matter, my own included. However, for readers not familiar with the subject, I offer below a succinct
account of this relatively new method, currently called ITC, which
seeks the electronic contact with hidden dimensions of life.

Life continues and the deceased go on living in another level that we
may call 'dimension' or 'world'. This is what the electronic voices tell us:
"everybody, all beings, survive physical death and transit into another world"
(Cardoso 2010, Locher and Harsch, 1989). Under certain circumstances,
not yet properly defined, the deceased (and also higher level, supra-human
beings) can be contacted through Instrumental Transcommunication.

The basic evidence provided by ITC, which supports the survival of
consciousness hypothesis, takes the form of voices, images and texts
produced on electronic media by methods still inexplicable by modern
science. I will deal mainly with the voices because my own research
focuses on these.

There are two types of anomalous electronic voices: the ones usually called EVP (Electronic Voice Phenomenon), which most of the time sound to the ear like human voices and appear recorded on magnetic tapes or digital devices, generally in reply to the operator's questions or comments. They can only be heard when the recording is played back. They may vary greatly in amplitude and intelligibility.

The other is known as DRV (Direct Radio Voices). These voices are much rarer and come directly into the air from the loudspeaker of a radio, usually also in response to questions or comments by the human operator. They may sound robotic and are often distorted. But when they are clear, they may allow for a dialogue and the reception of amazing information about "the other world", from where the voices proper state they have come.

Both EVP and DRV are apparently produced by invisible communicators who, for the most part, identify themselves as deceased humans. The messages received by both means, but mainly through the DRV, in some cases allow for lengthy conversations and cover a large spectrum of information – some of which may be previously unknown to the experimenter; from the identification of the communicator and other deceased personalities to descriptions of the next world or high ethical teachings.

Historically, the origin of audio ITC in its popular form, the well-known EVP, appears to go back to an American ethnographer, Waldemar Borogas, who in 1901 reported having accomplished the first registration of voices of unexplained origin during an expedition to Siberia, when recording the invocations of the shamans Chukchees. The ethnographer himself reported on the occurrence in *The Chukchee Jesup North Pacific Expedition*, Vol. 7, II, p. 435 (Grandsire 1998).

EVP voices, as we record them today, arose spontaneously and almost simultaneously in the 1950s in Italy, Sweden and the USA. Father Dr François Brune, a French theologian and renowned psychical researcher, reports in his best-seller *Les Morts Nous Parlent* (1988) that on the 17th of September 1952, two very eminent Catholic priests and academics, Fathers Drs Agostino Gemelli (a medical doctor and nuclear physicist) and Pellegrino Ernetti (a Benedictine from the famous Abbey of Saint Giorgio Maggiore in Venice) while working with Gregorian chants at the Experimental Laboratory of Physics of the Catholic University of Milan, recognized in one of the recordings the voice of Gemelli's father who reportedly addressed his son personally.

Taken aback by the occurrence, the two priests decided to bring the matter to the attention of Pope Pius XII. Amazingly, the Pope had a very positive reaction and reassured them on the nature of the occurrence, declaring, for the peace of mind of the two highly bewildered and concerned priests: "Do not worry Fathers! Your experience has nothing to do with Spiritism, for tape recorders cannot be influenced. It can even mark the beginning of a new scientific study to confirm the faith in the Afterlife" (Brune, 1993).

But it was the celebrated Swedish artist, opera singer and filmmaker Friedrich Jürgenson who is rightly called the great pioneer of the electronic voices. Not only did Jürgenson record several thousands of such communications commencing in 1959, but he also made his discovery famous in Europe and brought it to the attention of the world. A prominent figure in the European cultural circles of the mid-20th century, Jürgenson set aside his highly successful career and personal life to devote himself fully to the extraordinary discovery that totally changed his life (Jürgenson, 2004).

Although in 1956 EVP voices had already been recorded in the USA by Attila von Szalay in collaboration with Raymond Bayless (Rogo and Bayless, 1979), the Swedish artist knew nothing about the novel phenomenon and the American experimenters' results. With great intelligence, generosity and wisdom Friedrich Jürgenson, affectionately called Friedel by the voices, placed the phenomenon in the international arena, sparing no effort to achieve its recognition. He rightly deserves to be called 'the father of the electronic voices'.

One of the academics who read about his experiences was Dr Konstantin Raudive, a well-known Latvian philosopher with published work to his credit. Raudive started experimenting with Jürgenson and, although their ways parted a few years later, Raudive became a highly successful experimenter of his own right, being responsible for the rigorous, scientific approach that ITC phenomena earned in his time (see Raudive's excellent work *Breakthrough*, 1971).

Since its initial stage in the 1960s, a large amount of extraordinary material, which includes clear photos of deceased personalities, as well as long, direct dialogues and complex computer texts, was received by several researchers, particularly in continental Europe (Brune, 1993, 2005; Locher & Harsch 1989; Senkowski, 1995; Cardoso, 2010). It appears that some of the information regarding deceased individuals was unknown to anybody present during the experiments and its validity discovered by chance some time later. A number of ITC contacts of unprecedented significance were achieved mainly in Luxembourg by the couple Maggy and Jules Harsch-Fischbach and in Germany by Adolf Homes.

The communicators insisted on the objective nature of ITC and declared that their goal was to achieve direct contact with the operators, free from the interference of the minds of human mediums, with the aim of transmitting accurate information about their world and the purpose of life, to humans.

In my opinion, methods used in the past by communicators who affirm that they are from "the other world" have been fitting for the era concerned, and the same is now true of ITC. From the early part of the 20th century our civilization has quickly evolved into a technological society, based principally on electronics; ITC communications are mediated by electronic devices.

ITC contacts rapidly became well established and currently are producing an extensive range of what appears to be impressive evidence of survival of physical death. Furthermore, they provide us with objective phenomena of great value and significance in their own right, quite apart from their relevance to the survival hypothesis.

Chapter 2

SOME PRELIMINARY
REMARKS

Considering the number of comments and requests I receive from people around the world about the electronic voices, the question contained in the title of this book, *What do the voices tell us?* is one of the main concerns of people truly interested in the subject, independent of the reasons for their interest.

However, before getting into a discussion of the content of the anomalous electronic voices proper, allow me to put forward a few personal reflections about the reactions of people in general on the issue of anomalous electronic voices. Through them I hope to contribute to a better understanding of our subject of interest.

Sadly, the great majority of people consider the idea of "life after death", or "communications with the deceased" pure rubbish. They are not only ignorant of anything to do with purported communications from another dimension but, above all, they are not interested in finding out and this is perhaps the most important reason. As Ernesto Bozzano, one of the most eminent researchers of the survival of consciousness in the 19th century, pointed out, "the brain refutes the patterns that oppose deeply rooted convictions".

The same attitude is also true, although to a lesser extent, among those who grieve the passing of a loved one. Friedrich Jürgenson, the great pioneer of the anomalous electronic communications, had already commented that a significant majority of bereaved people are not truly interested in what, if anything, happened to their loved ones after death (Jürgenson, 2004). They are happy to forget about them, the sooner the better, and thus, escape the pain. This may seem cruel but if we analyze the facts objectively, as well as the bereavement situations we know of, we must admit that it is generally true.

And then, lastly, there are those few who are interested. I would divide the latter into two main groups: people who mourn because, having lost a dear one, they care, and those who have not lost anybody but are truly interested in life and all the unknown questions it raises.

There is still another small group constituted of a good majority of parapsychologists who are interested in psychic phenomena but refuse, *a priori*, the possibility of the continuation of consciousness beyond physical death mainly to please the orthodox scientific community, to which they endeavour to belong.

About the Voices Proper

One of the questions most frequently asked by the people who are interested in the electronic voices and the possibility of an afterlife, is directly related to the title of this work – what do the voices tell us? Before we proceed I need make some important remarks about the voices proper. Firstly, to explain that the electronic voices – and I am speaking of the Direct Radio Voices (DRV), the only ones that may allow an incipient dialogue – do not, in most cases, allow a fluid conversation between the experimenter on Earth and his or her partners from another dimension. We should keep this in mind.

With this clarification I wish to offer an anticipated reply to some of my readers' questions, which I assume will follow the same trend of the correspondence I receive on the subject. People write to me and ask if I could ask Rio do Tempo this or that? (Mostly about a deceased loved one). Normally I reply "I will try but I cannot guarantee that my communicators will be able to give me an answer." And this is the truth of the matter. The dialogue with the next world does not in most cases – with the exception, perhaps, of the amazing ITC contacts in Luxembourg and at Adolf Homes' in Germany of over twenty years ago – allow for the 'one question one straight reply' protocol. Exceptionally, however, they may do; this happened to me years ago, at the time when my main communicator, Carlos de Almeida, and I had long, frequent conversations, which sometimes complied with the protocol. But such cases are exceptional and the rule is very different. When I speak about the rule – and I must emphasize once more that this field has no established norms – I mean in the average ITC experimentation, including some of my own ITC contacts after Carlos de Almeida.

The Voices do not Resemble the Human Voices They Claim to Identify With

One very important point, and one which is brandished by sceptics to demonstrate the unreality of the voices or the fraud involved, or both, is the fact that, overall, the electronic voices do not resemble the voice of the deceased human they are supposed to belong to. Occasionally, however, they do.

People frequently ask me, "So your father spoke but could you recognize his voice?" Naturally, my straightforward reply, and I am speaking of the DRV, is that I could not – at least in the great majority of the cases. This is when I immediately see not only the disappointment but also the doubt in their eyes. I see them thinking "Well if the voice is not similar to her father's, it cannot be him speaking! Well, who knows what this stuff is all about?"

Although I must say that, on rare occasions, the voice did resemble my father's.

This point has been emphasized from the beginning of the DRV, and the reasons for it were explained later by the main architect of the splendid interdimensional contacts, the famous 'Technician', a high non-human entity that directed the communications in Luxembourg. The Technician explained that the voices are synthesized; this circumstance causes many of the problems to the reproduction of the exact characteristics of the human voices concerned. The Technician added that they endeavour to reproduce the latter as accurately as possible but, as we should expect, they do not always achieve perfection.

Once, a feminine voice that identified herself as Joan Colbert from Rio do Tempo Station, answered my question, "Can you tell me: how you produce your voices?" with "Damos-lhe a certeza que mascaramos; fazem-nos um sonograma" (You can be sure that we masquerade; they make us a sonogram) (See pertinent audio file in my 'Electronic

Voices' recording).[1] I think that the word 'masqueraded' should be understood in the sense that the voices we hear are not the communicators' real voices, which obviously they are not as they no longer have a physical voice. This reply fully corroborates the Luxembourg information about the voices being synthesized. The Technician assured Maggy Harsch-Fischbach that they would "try to synthesize the voice of the woman [her close friend Margret Mackes, who had died a couple of months before] as closely as possible" (Locher and Harsch, 1989).

The question of the similarity, or otherwise, of the anomalous voices carries so much weight (even for the earth experimenter) that ITC operator Adolf Homes, during a dialogue with a communicator, who identified himself as Professor Hans Bender, put the question directly to his interlocutor, "Herr Bender why do you speak with another voice?" and received from him this enigmatic reply:

> Only from your point of view are there clever and stupid individuals. Upper and lower awareness are identical. Both concepts are subjected to experienced concentration but no spectacle. The capability to mediate [between two dimensions] is the interest in oneself in conjunction with the Unknown and here 'many cooks spoil the broth' [an old German proverb meaning that 'many are not able to accomplish it']. What for you is paranormal is naturally effective. You can contact any being, because every spirit is present. Contact God, thus he logs in. So it is with Lucifer or another higher concept.

And the summary of that day ends with this extraordinary statement:

> ".... (Think), the clarity of the soul has at its disposal all knowledge. From my viewpoint, spiritual forms are also indescribable. Therefore, all things are possible in all dimensions." (Senkowski, ibid 1995, p.326).

My ITC communicator, Carlos de Almeida, corroborated this statement. At the very beginning of my ITC experiments, I once asked him through the DRV, "Carlos de Almeida can we expect to receive the transimages [anomalous electronic images]?"

His immediate, clear reply was "Podem tudo!" (You can [expect] everything!). We were then a small group of friends and so I, and he, spoke in the plural.

---

[1]   http://www.itcjournal.org/?product=electronic-voices-cd-in-mp3-format

Moreover, the deceased Konstantin Raudive is reported to have commented in Luxembourg, "It was said that the voices were not exactly the same. Friends, the paranormal cannot be repeated." (Schäfer ibid, p.106).

Conversely, Friedrich Jürgenson reports that he could often recognize the voices of individuals whom he knew well from their particular timbre and speech expressions. But Jürgenson was perhaps speaking of EVP voices and these seem to be more like the human ones. I must add that I have also recognized speech expressions and, to my great surprise, even the very special accent of Alentejo, the region in Portugal where I was born. But this is not exactly the topic of our discussion. The truth is that, overwhelmingly, the majority of the voices do not resemble the voices of the human personalities they claim to belong to. In view of the fact that the voices are synthesized, as we know they are, and because most of the time they sound synthetic, this is not at all surprising.

Similar Difficulties in Mediumship Contacts

Michael Tymn, the knowledgeable historian of psychical research, in his introduction to an 'interview' with Professor Hyslop, published in issue 47 of the *ITC Journal*, says this:

No doubt one of the reasons why research into mediumship has not been more widely accepted has to do with the lack of clarity in most of the communications purportedly coming from spirits. Even with the renowned mediums of yesteryear, such as Leonora Piper and Gladys Osborne Leonard, trance mediums who were frequently observed and tested by researchers and found to be genuine, there was much vagueness and ambiguity, even gibberish, in the communication. Sceptics saw all this as evidence that the so-called mediums were charlatans, as it was assumed that if spirits exist they could communicate in a much more intelligent manner. Clearly, communication with the spirit world is considerably more complex than a long-distance telephone call. The difficulty has been likened to prisoners tapping out messages to each other on the plumbing running between cells.

Certainly, the level of clarity of the messages has greatly improved with the ITC method but much of what Tymn points out, namely "...

it was assumed that if spirits exist they could communicate in a much more intelligent manner", still applies to the vast majority of the anomalous electronic messages. We will get into this point later in the book but I must refer here to an important situation put forward by the communicating entities, i.e. "we [here on the earth] only receive in our dimension fractions of the contacts they send us" (Senkowski, 1995).

I can personally corroborate this with a good example of my own experimentation. Years ago, my main communicator, Carlos de Almeida, had a dialogue with me of over an hour and a half. This was an extraordinary happening because his voice was clear and very loud and I asked him the most important questions any sensitive human being can think of. I interrogated him on life issues of transcendental nature, which I have longed to know about all my adult life. He always replied but I could not understand what he said directly. I did not mind because I thought I would be able to understand his replies once I put the audio file into my computer and listened with the sound editing software. The voice was very loud – it could be heard at the end of my 3.000 sq meters garden while I was in my studio at the opposite point of the garden – but it had great echo. I thought this would not matter once I worked on it with the software. However, it did matter and I still could not understand a full sentence of what he said; only a word here and there.

In a desperate attempt to find a solution that would release such important information, I took the tape to a professional recording and sound editing studio and asked them to analyse the sound track. A few days later the studio called me to pick up the tape. I went over and met a puzzled sound technician. He asked me what kind of recording was this because they could make no sense at all of the speech. He added that the masculine talk was formed by what seemed to be truncated words, i.e. a syllable followed by another syllable which did not connect with the previous one and so on. It was as if there were speech fractions missing in the words. He said it was a very strange recording.

Naturally I had not told the sound technician what the tape was about. This happened in Galicia, the northwest region of Spain where I live. A place where everybody understands Portuguese well because the local language is the Galician, a dialect of the Portuguese, and Portugal is just 30 km away from Virgo. To this day I could not solve the mystery of Carlos de Almeida's long replies to my many difficult questions. I cried in frustration over such an extraordinary, albeit lost, opportunity! I must add that, as usual, my radios were tuned to white noise frequencies where no voices could ever be heard and that Carlos de Almeida's customary voice addressed me personally.

Going back to Mike Tymn, he quotes several other cases that illustrate the difficulties involved in the so-called spirit communication. And I again quote from the above mentioned paper:

> Soon after his death in 1925, Sir William Barrett, a physicist and pioneering psychical researcher, began communicating with his wife, Dr. Florence Barrett through medium Gladys Osborne Leonard. At a sitting on November 5, 1929, Barrett communicated;

> When I come into the conditions of a sitting I then know that I can only bring with me – contain in me – a small portion of my consciousness. The easiest things to lay hold of are what we may call ideas; a detached word, a proper name, has no link with a train of thought except in the detached sense; that is far more difficult than any other feat of memory or association of ideas. ... (Barrett, 1937, p. 105).

I know that he is speaking of mediumistic communications and we are dealing here with ITC ones, which are more objective and, for that reason, accepted as more reliable. However, there have been in the world, mainly in times past, top-class mediums who were responsible for some of the most comprehensive communications from another dimension ever received on this planet. Gladys Osborne Leonard was one of them. But the important point now is that what the deceased Sir William Barrett purportedly said fits what we know from modern ITC communications. Above all are the difficulties involved, constantly reiterated by our communicators, and the concentration required for conveying their messages. A short time ago, a voice that identified itself as my father's said (translation) "We are in a dream [state] here!"

Could this be comparable to Sir William Barrett's "I can only carry with me – contain in me – a small portion of my consciousness"? I suppose so.

In addition, I must stress one very important point related to this issue as ITC operators we cannot summon anybody in the next dimension to speak with us at will. It may happen that the person we want to speak to will reply (or somebody on his or her behalf); we have no clear way of knowing which one but, more likely, it will happen that we get no answer. Sometimes we may have just a short reply saying that it is not possible to speak with that person. Again, in this field there are no rules we may rely on.

To give you an example, I will go over the story of some of the requests I made to my communicators. At the beginning of my experimentation I used to insist on speaking with my father, João Cardoso. One day I said "Why doesn't my father communicate? How is it possible that he cannot speak with me?" And I continued "He appeared to be psychically gifted during his lifetime in this world, so I think that he must be in a better position to communicate."

The youngest son of a traditional, highly conservative Portuguese family that did not even recognize the existence of such things, my father had, nevertheless, experienced what are now called Out of Body Experiences (OBEs) all his life, and had a few remarkable incidents of retro-cognition. I had received no reply whatsoever to my constant queries about my father but, on that occasion, a voice immediately replied to my remark and said "Well, that's what you think!" Thus, the fact of having been 'psychically gifted' – as parapsychologists used to call it – does not seem to influence the capacity of speaking to our world from the next dimension. Fortunately, in more recent years, since the time of Carlos de Almeida, my father has spoken many times and has now become my main communicator.

Content of the Transmessages

For easier understanding I will divide this section into topics. The communicators' recorded direct replies or comments will be between inverted commas. Although running the risk of not making much sense in proper English, I offer literal translations of the electronic communications. I believe this is safer than involuntarily changing the meaning of the messages, which, by and large, are in Portuguese. My remarks, and the conclusions I sometimes reach on the issues we are discussing, are based on the direct speech of the voices. I will clearly indicate when, instead of a logical observation based on the information directly received from the voices, a speculation of my own making applies.

Information I perceived mentally will be in normal writing. I do ask my readers, however, not to take the latter at face value. I could have made mistakes in interpretation. Information I receive telepathically is not always accurate. Sometimes I do perceive things incorrectly, while at other times the information is absolutely right and it can be verified independently. This is a very elusive field, even more so than the anomalous electronic voices because the latter, provided they are clear and loud, can be verified objectively.

Throughout the book I will quote and translate Adolf Homes' tran-stexts: the anomalous messages which appeared on his computer screen, or in his floppy disks, without his intervention and sometimes even when he was not at home and his computer was turned off (See Senkowski, 1995). I will also quote extensively the Luxembourg contacts received by Maggy and Jules Harsch-Fischbach. Professor Ernst Senkowski ob-served Adolf Homes' contacts closely and directly, as well as Maggy and Jules Harsch-Fischbach's work. He was present and participated in numerous communications in Luxembourg. Dr Senkowski was a priv-ileged interlocutor of the Dr Swejen Salter of Zeitstrom (Timestream) group, the otherworld station in direct contact with the Luxembourg group (Senkowski, ibid 1995).

Chapter 3

THE NATURAL LAW

I believe that the unknown, probably infinite, nature hides the secret of these extraordinary communications. At the Bacci Centre in Grosseto,[2] I witnessed a beautiful DRV message pronounced by the entity that the Italian experimenters call Gregorio, which said (in the Italian original): *"Dove vai errando Bacci, in questo universo niente perisce, cambia semplicemente la forma, la legge della natura che governa questo regno perverra' alla conoscenza del tutto."* (Where are you wandering Bacci, in this universe nothing perishes it simply changes the shape, the Law of Nature that governs this realm will arrive at the understanding of the whole.) (See ITC Journal 21, 2005).

Very recently, I was thrilled to find that some of Adolf Homes' outstanding anomalous computer texts expressly address the issue of the Natural Law and its relationship to the ITC communications we receive today. The compilation by Professor Ernst Senkowski is organized by topics. Below, I translate one of those:

---

[2] Marcello Bacci is a famous Italian ITC experimenter whom I have visited a few times in his experimentation centre in Grosseto, Italy (See Cardoso, 2010).

Law – Compliance with the Natural Law

The collective self is built upon the basis of the law of harmony of everything that exists. The global existence of all living beings creates the respective compliance of law in the structures. In love and again [we say] in love stands the basic law of all that is. The spiritually created universal harmony law of all the beings in all the worlds creates any materialization. All the dramas of your life, either negative or positive, are based upon this law. Your system is not at all perfect. It does not make any difference if you help each other or if you kill each other. You are not able to change the law. Some of you receive information from other areas of consciousness in which different laws are at work. Even I, here, am submitted to the Natural Law and am working with other phenomena which I cannot yet penetrate. Other data from me are not unfortunately possible: the compliance should be respected. The basic essence of life is to release fully what for you is transient. [Note: The last sentence is a free translation of the German phrase: *"Endsorgung des für Sie Vergänglichen ist, ist die Grundsubstanz des Lebens"*].

Cycle Within the Meaning of the Established Laws.

Love is in harmony with the Natural Law. The Omnipotence's compliance with the Natural Law created the free will of all life. By virtue of the respect due to the compliance with the Natural Law, we have little impact on the physical being. The similarities between your and our physical laws reside in the cosmic compliance with the Natural Law. All the contacts with other forms of consciousness are based upon the cosmic compliance with the Natural Law. Identification with us through compliance with the Natural Law: research, knowledge, patience, humility and love." (Senkowski, German original p. 34, Italian p. 68. 1999).

Some of the affirmations contained here, e.g. "The Omnipotence's compliance with the Natural Law created the free will of all life" are very difficult to take at face value. Where is, for instance, the free will of a blade of grass or a little mouse that we, humans, use and abuse in our laboratories? Unless, of course, it exists at a much deeper cosmic level, one which we cannot envisage and even less assess. We, humans, should realize that we do not understand most of life's ways, although, regrettably, we think we do.

But as early as the mid-19th century the entities that contacted us from the next dimension of life had already hinted at the subject we are discussing – the Natural Law.

Judge W. Edmonds, Chief Justice of the New York State Supreme Court, is believed to have been the first true psychical researcher. This prominent personality started his meticulous investigations of mediumistic communications in 1851 and finally published *Spiritualism Volumes I and II* with George T. Dexter, MD. One of his questions to the communicating entities was "What is this which I am witnessing? Is it a departure from nature's laws or in conformity with them? Is it a miracle, or is it the operation of some hitherto unknown but pre-existing cause, now for the first manifesting itself?" He received the following answer, "It is the result of human progress, it is an execution, not a suspension, of nature's laws, and it is not now for the first time manifesting itself, but in all ages of the world has at times been displayed." (See *ITC Journal* 48, June 2014, p. 74).

As our communicators have stated, thoughts and concepts live and through them we have constructed an image of the world, which seems to be totally misguided. This is perhaps the reason that prevents us from seeing beyond the veil that separates dimensions. As William Blake so splendidly put it: "If the doors of perception were cleansed, everything would appear to man as it is, Infinite. For man has closed himself up, till he sees all things thro' narrow chinks of his cavern."

Maybe this is the reason why Rio do Tempo has told me that animals are more aware of the existence of their world than humans. The intellect might very well prove to be not our glory but our curse.

I believe that, as a species, we humans need a great deal of humility and introspective capacity to be able to acknowledge that we have created artificial, misguided concepts, which have become our guiding stars but which are nothing more than misconstructions on the fundamental issues of life and of our role in the world. Power, in whatever shape, has become the main attribute of our behaviour and has replaced compassion, sense of duty, respect and, of course, love. We invented the law of separateness to replace the law of wholeness, the Natural Law. In its place we inserted different, minor laws, which are bound to become fatal because they only serve human interests and purposes, not the interests of the whole. But in the next world the laws seem to be much more in tune with the Natural Law. We need to learn a lot when we get there.

Survival is Universal

Together with "There is another world, there is another way", the message that survival is universal is the main information from Rio do Tempo communications. Survival is not ruled by ethical, religious, or any other requisites. It is merely a fact of life. It is inevitable.

When, many years ago, I asked Carlos de Almeida, my main communicator, as I said, "What happens to plants?" he replied "Don't forget that plants are beings of your world; from the other world [ours] all transit into this world [theirs]".

I consider that I am not a person with preconceptions, at least the usual ones. However, I must admit that when Carlos de Almeida forcefully answered me as above I was stunned. I think this happened in 1998 and I had not yet read any ITC literature that could have influenced my interpretation of the voice's content. Besides, the reply, although soft, was clear and there was no margin for doubt about the interpretation. I did not hide this information and spoke about it in conferences and papers, but certain uneasiness remained with me for some time. Naturally, some critics who read my papers made fun of it, joking about the survival of the lettuce and the carrot.

Carlos de Almeida's information prompted me to explore the issue of plants, beings that I love greatly. I already knew of Cleve Backster's work, albeit very superficially, but then I discovered the writings of Sir Jagdish Chandra Bose and was fascinated. My Rio do Tempo information now started to make sense, from the scientific point of view and also from the point of view of consciousness. My communicators had told me about consciousness (literal translation), "All beings in the world have consciousness".

It was all to do with the survival of consciousness, I thought. To tell the truth I never asked my communicators about the survival of minerals, but I suppose the same rule applies. Besides, minerals concentrate, and are a source of, great energy, and energy cannot die.

Among the hundreds of computer texts received by Adolf Homes, and the high teachings they convey, there is also extraordinary information about living beings' and minerals' lives. Here is one of those teachings:

... All that lives, and everything lives, is part of creation. Concepts live, the dead live, computers live, everything lives. Every life is fulfilled through transformation. Every life in the worlds, even the most diverse, searches [for] unlimited perfection ...

And specifically about minerals:

... Every life – animal, plant, mineral, and all kinds of coarse matter as well as subtle matter – consists solely and absolutely of information." (Senkowski, 1999, German orig p. 49; Italian translation p. 132).

Interestingly, the same superior beings stated this about the different forms of life: ".... we do not need your electromagnetic technique to switch your instruments on because silicon, nerve cell and consciousness are absolutely the same thing for us..." (Senkowski, ibid, German original p. 19; Italian translation p. 40. 1999). And again on page 38 of the original and 61 of the Italian edition, "Our request to you is that of identifying yourselves with your planet and all life in it because everything of you is formed of identical elementary particles. To us silicon, nerve cell and consciousness are absolutely identical..."

What an extraordinary affirmation, which totally contradicts one of our main paradigms, the one that associates consciousness with biological life and, even more shortsightedly, with *only* some forms of it! We definitely need to discard our traditional mental patterns and prejudices, and look at these mysterious messages with a mind as open as possible. It is not an easy task, but, in order fully to absorb the astounding communications we have been privileged to receive, it is an urgent and indispensable one.

The Survival of Plants and Human Anthropocentrism

Speaking about the survival of plants, I must say that I have read many reports on ITC experiences and mediumship communications, although the latter much less thoroughly. Very few of them, for example, the exceptional Homes' messages, refer to the survival of other species i.e., the non-human ones. There are exceptions, in general dogs and a few other animals, but mostly in the scope of their relationships with humans.

I never fail to be baffled by the abhorrent anthropocentrism that characterizes this attitude. Why should we be amazed, for instance, at the survival of plants? What is the criterion behind this attitude? Are we puzzled by their existence in this dimension? Of course we are not; then, why would we be surprised at their survival in another dimension? Notwithstanding the fact that plants are the foundation of life on this planet, and this is a very important reason.

But what is truly at the bottom of such absurd approach? I am sure that the excuse will be consciousness. I mean people in general will say that plants are not conscious beings. But do they really know what they are talking about? Just because a plant, or a mouse, a bee, a butterfly, etc. are different from us, are we to assume that they are not conscious beings? We can only say that their consciousness appears to be different from human consciousness; and that is really all we can say.

Furthermore, and specifically in regard to plants, Professor Stefano Mancuso, currently one of the highest authorities in the world on vegetable neurophysiology, author of *Brilliant Green: The Surprising History and Science of Plant Intelligence,* maintains that plants are not only intelligent and conscious beings but that they, in many respects, also exceed humans.

Speaking about Mancuso, I recently found a passage of his work that made me shiver because I had felt something similar a long time ago. It said "When we smell the perfume of a flower, we smell its message". He was referring to the plants' communication with insects, while I have had strange experiences regarding the perfume of flowers in a different context – plants seemed to respond to my benign and loving thoughts about them by sending me their scent. I mean, they were not particularly fragrant flowers and I could only feel their perfume after I had thought fondly about them and sometimes even at a distance. I was puzzled but did not give it further consideration. However, at a certain point, after the same thing happened to me over and over again, I wondered if they were indeed responding to my feelings and to the telepathic messages I was sending them. Naturally, I cannot be sure of anything, but it is possible. They are intelligent and sensitive beings, so why not?

The arrogant, to a great extent western-influenced, attitude that considers humankind superior to all other life forms on this planet greatly influences the way we think about other beings, and plants in particular. Nevertheless, at Adolf Homes' one of the communicating high entities guaranteed that:

> ... the man has the same fate of the animal. Both breathe the same air. Both travel the same road. None has advantage. Both are made of dust and into dust will turn. The last breath of both goes in the same direction. The only difference is that the man can exploit the animal and not vice-versa ...

For my part I cannot resist adding that, sadly, this may be the only difference but it is also an enormous one that causes incalculable suffering; something which is never taken into consideration in any assessment of human activities.

The Role of Religions in Human Anthropocentrism

At a more common level, here in the western world where I live, the surprise of so-called normal people at the survival of non-human animals (in this context I would not even dare mention the survival of plants...) seems to be based on a religion-oriented view. Indeed, religions, particularly the monotheistic ones, play a huge role in this disgraceful situation. They have created a God in the image of man and this has had tremendous implications that threaten life and all its manifestations. It contains the seeds of unstoppable destruction and, ultimately, self-destruction.

Humans see their technological and scientific success stories as tools of supremacy and, consequently, as examples of superiority. However, I postulate that this is foolish and short-sighted because, for example, how can the construction of a dam that destroys a river and all life in it be a sign of superior intelligence? Isn't the intelligence of the beaver that lives in total harmony with the river and sustainably uses the resources it offers more admirable?

Camille Flammarion, the eminent French astronomer, remarked that there are people who believe that bays exist for boats to anchor in them, moonlight to delight the romantics, flowers to bring joy to our lives, etc. In my opinion, this is the point of the question. The human view of life and of all the other species is entirely anthropocentric and anthropomorphic. All that matters is that which is important from a human point of view and not of itself. We evaluate other species systematically from our human perception, never from a planetary or universal one. Nothing could be more wrong or more unfair and dangerous. Naturally our attitude draws from the power we have over all the other animals, vegetables and minerals.

From their side, religions grant a sacred basis to the evolutionary turn that put man at the top of the planetary life ladder; they proclaim it as a gift of God to Man. But let's ponder briefly the power that effectively we possess over the other species – does power represent an ethical basis for whatever decision or action? Does power justify unlimited abuse, exploitation and cruelty? Obviously it does not. Certainly we, as humankind, still have a long way to go to deserve the power that evolution, randomly or by cosmic design, has bestowed upon us.

Chapter 4

WE ARE DEALING WITH
ANOTHER DIMENSION

Naturally, when we discuss anomalous electronic communications we are forced to deal with the challenging difficulty of thinking about situations and events outside our dimension. But how can we, logically, achieve such thinking? I suggest we cannot. However, people, ITC operators included, try to 'adapt' the information we receive about that unknown dimension to our known conditions on this planet. Although I fully understand their reasons, which are only natural, I reckon that this is misleading and may create unnecessary confusion, which adds to the ridicule our contacts are bombarded with daily.

On one memorable occasion, at the end of a beautiful chant by a masculine and feminine choir from Rio do Tempo station, a powerful masculine voice announced loudly "We are from another dimension, we are from beyond time." And on another occasion, "We speak from the other level; humans need to know about the Light." These utterances and others can be listened to on my audio recording '*Electronic Voices*'[3]

Certainly many aspects of the complex situation of dealing with another dimension – a concept still rejected by present-day science – will

---

[3] http://www.itcjournal.org/?product=electronic-voices-cd-in-mp3-format

remain obscure and many questions will remain unanswered. For now, we have no way of clarifying those topics further; we simply have no answers for them. Thus, I will convey the information I and other ITC operators have received from our communicators whilst trying not to interpret it from the point of view of our circumstances in this dimension. Often the contents of ITC messages are incredibly mindboggling.

The Difficult Task of Communicating With Our World

One of the most important points that we need to keep in mind when we analyse the interaction between two dimensions through ITC are the difficulties involved. It seems that communication with our world is a very difficult, strenuous job for our ITC partners. My own communicators have reiterated over and over how difficult it is for them to speak with us, here, in this world. In fact, at the end of his first DRV contact with me, Carlos de Almeida shouted "This is very, very difficult! Another world!" and then his voice vanished. (See DRV example 1 of the CD).

Many years later, a guttural voice, apparently from my paternal grandfather, who seems to be very involved in the ITC Bridge that Rio do Tempo has established with my house, clearly acknowledged it. The masculine voice, which by the end of that evening contact had become husky, uttered slowly and heavily, with great difficulty, "This is the voice of effort!" before suddenly becoming silent.

Furthermore, considering that the communicating entities have confirmed that we hear their thoughts, it is easy to imagine the tremendous effort of concentration they need use to modulate static radio noise into coherent human speech to produce the DRV. Once more, the *modus faciendi* to accomplish the transformation is unknown to us.

I believe also that there must be many other factors involved in the process of achieving a contact with us. The Luxembourg experimenter Maggy Harsch-Fischbach remarked about the first telephone call she received from the deceased Nobel Prize winner Konrad Lorenz:

> ...Conversely to those who are incapable of expressing themselves verbally or those who learn the communication rules with great difficulty only, Konrad Lorenz seems not to have any difficulty in 'transforming' his thoughts, with the aid of devices [other world instruments], into human language. (Harsch and Locher, French edition, 1995, p. 209).

The reference to the use of other world devices is very interesting but we must bear in mind that Timestream communicators had informed the experimenters that their devices are of a different nature from ours. Similarly, not only are their devices of a different nature, their bodies and everything else in the next dimension is of a different nature also. It seems that, in the next dimension, consciousness is more visibly the creator of matter than in our world; matter is subtler than on the earth but is still matter, although of a finer kind.

The issue of devices, which apparently facilitate the communication process in the next world, inevitably draws us into the subject of energy.

Energy in the Scope of ITC Contacts

When we analyze the anomalous electronic voices, it is easy to confirm that energy saving appears to direct the course of their speech, which is, in general, free of superfluous terms and statements. However, to venture into the definition of which kind or kinds of energy are used to transmit their messages is another matter, and I am unable to offer anything of value in this field. I think that most likely this involves different energies, which are unknown to us. I am using the term 'energy' in the widest possible sense and beyond what we normally call energy in our world. Of course I cannot identify those types of energy because they do not fit into our current understanding of energy, which is predominantly physical. Emotional and mental energies, for instance, could be among those used.

Actually, the communicators have hinted at some possibilities. In Luxembourg the experimenters asked Timestream what kind of energy they worked with, and Swejen Salter, one of the most active members at Timestream station, informed them, "We work with Orgone energy. Ask Professor Senkowski to explain it to you. We use also 'energy residues' but they are pure positive energies deprived of human influences."

At Adolf Homes' the communicators referred to 'Od energy' – the life force experimented with and demonstrated by Baron Carl von Reichenbach, very similar to Reich's Orgone energy, which ancient cultures called Chi, Prana, etc. Below are excerpts of what they conveyed at Homes':

...The contact connections can be prevented by a too feeble radiating energy on the part of those who receive them. You call it force of Od.

As you know, the totality of the human body possesses an energy, which you understand as electrophysiological energy. During a transcontact we influence the physical fields known to you using the following energies and their respective fields: unstable electrostatic – electrophysiology – mystical – radar – telepathy. Your measurements of them are not correct. The radar energy has nothing to do with yours. In regard to tachyons, we are dealing with pure forms of energy ... (Senkowski, *Transkommunikation*, Special issue, Vol. IV, Sonderheft 1999, Italian translation pp. 26 and 43 respectively).

During the laborious investigations carried out by George Meek to obtain data that would allow the reception of electronically transmitted transcendental information from superior beings, the group of investigators he had assembled were told the following on the issue of energy:

The problem is to put the energies we work with together to produce the voice sound. Our work is done mainly through thought or mind energies ... There can be the combination of certain energies to create voice. (Fuller, 1985, p. 67).

Once again, we see that the communicators said "certain energies" without specifying what they were.

My Rio do Tempo communicators have not specifically mentioned the issue of energy but, on several occasions, the voice that was speaking to me uttered suddenly, in a sinking tone "Oh, my voice is going..." and that was the end of that evening's contact.

I suspect these forces – if indeed they function the way we would expect them to, which I doubt, are just a component of a much more complex system, which we are not able to understand at our present phase of development. My supposition is based solely on the observation of the electronic voices and the way they develop, as well as on the few remarks the communicators have made on these issues. Nevertheless, it seems to be confirmed by some extraordinary definitions of energy received by Adolf Homes mostly in the form of the anomalous computer texts that I have been citing. For instance, some of those messages stated:

From our side there is exchange of energy and fusion of energy of the spirit, of thoughts and of sentiments thanks to acceleration not influenced by gravitation.

And:

... Your concept of energy form does not correspond unequivocally to our reality. In our systems your current energy requirements are not necessary ...

And thirdly:

We are the deceased who have assembled in groups to render new energies usable. Using all our intensity, new forms of energy are created. The energies with which we move are not noticeable to you. The transcontacts take place through concentrated fluxes of energy. Energy, independent from its form, is important for instrumental contacts. (Senkowski, ibid *Transkommunikation*, Italian translation p. 43).

Transkommunikation, a magazine founded by the German physicist Professor Ernst Senkowski, published a special issue on Adolf Homes' contacts. It contains a richness of material of great interest on every subject matter, laboriously assembled and organized by Dr Senkowski. However, unfortunately for the English readers, the publication is in German with a translation only into Italian. I must emphasize that Adolf Homes was a modest carpenter of limited formal education, who often could not understand the content of the texts he received and relied on Dr Senkowski for clarification. I received this information personally from Professor Senkowski.

Frequency and Vibration

Again at Adolf Homes', the transcendental entities focused on two fundamental factors in the communication process. However, once more, we should be aware that the terms used – *frequency* and *vibration* – do not correspond to what we call frequency and vibration. In his analysis of the content of some of Homes' messages, Professor Senkowski puts it this way:

While the transentities unusual use of the concept of 'energy' can be fairly accepted [by us], frequency (and vibration) totally diverge from our current concepts. Neither the general meaning 'frequency of events' nor the physics/ technical definition - 'number of oscillations in a given time' correspond to 'psychic frequencies' [a concept] unknown to us. (Senkowski, ibid Italian translation p. 60).

And the communicating entities confirm this:

Our frequency has nothing to do with your electro-magnetic waves. These spectra of light, these frequencies, appear then by you as acoustic signals or, possibly, even as optical signals. ... "

And also this:

Light is spirit and information. Energies of light penetrate all physical as well as psychical forms. Light, which you cannot measure, is not composed of electro-magnetic radiation. It has nothing to do with your electro-magnetic waves. We are faster than the speed of your light.

I translate below some comments by the same entities about '*vibration*', a fundamental element to achieve the contact:

... The points of coordination are nothing more than the result of a vibration which equals ours. From your side a greater psychic vibration is necessary. Through pluri-dimensional effects, you reach a higher vibration. The basic information is always correct; it is only the difference of vibration of the moment that deforms (and obstructs) it. If between two systems there is a too strong diversity of vibration, the possibility exists that the genuine information will be deformed or even falsified. We receive positive vibrations from many experimenters. We recognize the vibrations which indicate your availability. Feeble vibrations originated from more than one of the experimenters (in a group experiment) are reinforced thanks to some of those present endowed with greater mediumship.

Several experimenters are not in vibration synchronization with their apparatus. Only few of you find – through the instruments – the frequency of vibration suitable to us, which can link together different structures. Vibration harmonization with your instruments renders our contacts possible. Two-way contacts cease with the death of the experimenter because the necessary vibration no longer exists ... (Senkowski ibid, Italian translation, p. 131).

The above explanations are very important in themselves and also because one usual accusation against the electronic contacts is precisely that the contacts end with the death of the ITC operator who received them. This happened most noticeably with William O'Neil and the Spiricom project and was the main reason that stirred accusations of falsity and fraud against O'Neil. The Spiricom was intended to be a venture available to anyone who would like to contact other dimensions of life; however, it never reached that stage very likely due to the death of its operator, William O'Neil. I highly recommend the reading of Fuller's excellent book to anyone interested in ITC and all the vicissitudes this discipline has gone through (Fuller, ibid 1985).

Perhaps some of the reasons above explain the reply I received from my own communicators when I asked them why they normally spoke through one of my five radios. "Because that is the radio you like most," they said. And this was true but it is also true that, years later, they stopped speaking through that radio and started using another one instead. As I typically say: rules are useless in this field! Our rules certainly are.

Chapter 5

PERMISSION IS REQUIRED

From what the voices tell us, there is a requirement for our ITC contacts to take place – our communicators need permission to make them. Interestingly, I have also seen the issue of 'authorization' mentioned in several trustworthy works on mediumship communications.

I emphasize once more that all quotes I offer my readers in this book are based upon the most impeccable and honest works I was able to find. This means that I will not quote from the Internet or from books whose authors do not provide guarantee of truthfulness and rigor. And if, sometimes, I cannot recall the source of the mediumship citations, for example, I guarantee that they will be from books by some of the most outstanding international investigators of psychic phenomena. The majority of them belong to the British SPR, a prestigious institution that counted a number of Nobel Prize winners among its members, directors and researchers.

Oscar D'Argonnel's Book on Telephone Calls From the Beyond and Modern ITC

Going back to ITC proper, I made a discovery some time ago, when I received a valuable gift from two lovely young Brazilian friends. Sergio

Bonilha and Luciana Ohira were in Galicia and they invited me to give a presentation on ITC at the University of La Coruña where they were doing research on the influence of the invisible in Art.

Their gift was a rare little book called *Vozes do Além pelo Telefone* (*Voices from the Beyond by the Telephone*) by Oscar D' Argonnel, a highly desirable report, greatly sought after by ITC researchers. I had heard of the book but never thought I would one day be able to read it. I was delighted beyond words because, published in 1925, it is extremely difficult to find. Apparently this is the first published report on anomalous telephone calls.

Oscar D' Argonnel was a Portuguese-Brazilian researcher, knowledgeable and highly interested in 'experimental Spiritism' (as it was called at the time). He observed and studied Spiritualist phenomena with a critical and unbiased eye. Remarkably, he was also a non-religious man who criticized the dogmas and the claims of 'truth holders' made by the followers of the different creeds, including Spiritism. It is obvious from reading this book that D' Argonnel was a serious, distinguished investigator first and foremost, interested in testing the veracity of the alleged anomalous phenomena of Spiritism with the goal of advancing his quest for the truth about the survival hypothesis. He vehemently stated, almost one hundred years ago, that "objective demonstration is an indispensable factor to accept the veracity of the phenomena of Spiritualism". I confess that I could not agree more! He authored other books which, unfortunately, I cannot get.

Among D' Argonnel's observations. I found many similarities to our current ITC experiences. One was the case of the compulsory permission to speak to our world from the next dimension. On page 21 of the above-mentioned work, D' Argonnel quotes from one of the many anomalous telephone conversations he received. His other world communicator said "... we have severe laws here and today I cannot speak to her [a family member who was by the telephone wanting to speak with the communicating entity]".

On pages 39-40, he again quotes the same entity as saying "I have already warned you, D' Argonnel that this phenomenon cannot be shown to anybody without the chief's permission; orders here are very strict and must be obeyed to the letter. You have ignored my recommendations and therefore, you are going to be deprived of this new system of communication". On that occasion, D' Argonnel had allowed a group of friends to listen with him to the beautiful loud chants he was receiving through the telephone. And again on page 45, his communicator says

"... I had no permission to do that. I have told you [D' Argonnel] that we cannot do anything here without permission from above".

On page 59: "Constante [the name of a friend] asked me to tell you that he would be greatly pleased to speak frequently with you and his son, but he must obey the laws of the spiritual world". The clarity of the above recommendations leaves no doubt about their meaning.

Moreover, we should pay attention to the three main points mentioned by the communicating entity: the indispensable "permission from above", the existence of "laws in the spirit world" and the reference to "the new system of communication", or ITC. The latter statement obviously implies that, at the time, at the beginning of our 20th century, the communicators already spoke of a "system of communication", which means an organized structure for the contacts with our world. References to this "new system of communication", which was being developed in the next world, were systematically received in our world through several channels, namely mediumistic ones (see Cardoso, 2010 p. 27; Grandsire, 1998). But D' Argonnel's seems to be the first direct and explicit categorization of the phenomena.

When, years ago, at the beginning of my reception of the DRVs I heard a voice categorically say "They are putting laws for everything here." I could not believe my ears and, although the voice was clear, I was so baffled by the content that my mind refused it. I did not hide it but avoided speaking about this particular message for fear of the ridicule and disbelief it would certainly cause in people to whom I revealed it. If I myself could not believe my ears, what about other people, I thought.

And then, to my great surprise, several years later I saw the issue of permission mentioned in the scope of other anomalous communications, e.g. mediumistic ones and, very recently, in the precious first little book *A new admirable communication system: The spirits speak via telephone* by Oscar D' Argonnel.

There are many other similarities between D' Argonnel's report and modern ITC voices, including the type of noises made by the telephone during the contacts and other acoustic characteristics of the electronic voices. A number of situations described in this report are reproduced almost literally in many modern ITC messages, mine included, almost one hundred years later. And again I offer that the striking similarities between ITC messages, so separated by latitude and distant in time, are the best confirmation of the independent existence of the next world and of a common pattern prevailing in, at least, some aspects of life in that world. This is the case of the rules that govern the contacts with our own world, among others.

More recently than D' Argonnel, at the home of the Luxembourg experimenters, Jules and Maggy Harsch-Fischbach, one of the main communicators from 'Zeitstrom' Station, Dr Swejen Salter, said on the same subject:

> Unfortunately I cannot and I should not reply to all the questions. Do not forget that I need to request the permission of superior beings for some messages. (Locher and Harsch, 1992, p. 168, Portuguese edition).

If permission to speak with our world appears to be an obligatory requirement, the topics covered during these interdimensional contacts seem to be highly controlled as well. I have mentioned the strong voice that warned "Not to that!" in reply to a question I had asked, but there were other occasions when I got the clear impression that my communicators could not speak about certain matters. Like, for instance, when a masculine voice announced very loudly "I am João Cardoso!" and immediately another voice reprimanded, "You don't have to say that [his name]; only Rio do Tempo!" João Cardoso was my father's name (Example 15 of the CD or MP3, 'Electronic Voices').[4] This was one of the first voices I recorded pronouncing my father's name. After that and until today, a masculine voice has uttered my father's name innumerable times. But maybe he has been granted permission since then. Of course I do not know for sure but I believe it is a possibility.

ITC Communication Confirms Some of Allan Kardec's Teachings

The remark by the second voice that warned my father not to say his name could also be related to one of the most significant aspects of life in the next world, the Group-Soul, as we will see in a subsequent chapter.

On this issue Allan Kardec, the well-known founder of Spiritism, is quoted as offering as early as the 19th century:

> In proportion, as spirits are purified and elevated in the hierarchy, the distinctive characters of their personality are, in some way, obliterated in the uniformity of perfections, and yet they do not preserve their individuality any less. This is the case with the superior and with the

---

[4]   http://www.itcjournal.org/?product=electronic-voices-cd-in-mp3-format

pure spirits. In this condition, the name they had on earth, in one of their thousand ephemeral corporeal existences, is quite an insignificant thing. Let us remark again that spirits are attracted to each other by the similarity of their qualities, and that they thus form sympathetic groups or families. (*ITC Journal* 50, p. 57).

Apparently, work and tasks in the next level of life represent a common venture in which all participate. And I specifically know this to be true, at least in regard to the endeavour to contact our world, as the loud voices I record clearly state it. Thus, if the production of the anomalous electronic voices is the result of collective, strenuous labour and invention, and the voices we hear are not the real voices of the communicating entities but a synthetic reproduction of human speech that involves everybody, as explained elsewhere (see Cardoso, 2010), the request of non-identification appears right and understandable.

Going back to the issue of permission, I will tell my readers that once, in the middle of a dialogue between myself and an anomalous voice that had identified itself as my grandmother's, a different voice suddenly interrupted to say "You may continue!" apparently allowing the initial voice to carry on the conversation with me.

Furthermore, I think that, with very few exceptions, e.g., the Luxembourg contacts (supervised by the Technician) as well as many communications received by Adolf Homes – and both situations seemed to be under the control of superior beings – the triviality, which undoubtedly characterizes many anomalous communications, is the direct result of the lack of permission to address more elevated issues.

Another impression we get clearly from the content of ITC messages is that our hierarchies are not relevant in the next world. This point is illustrated in many different ways. For example, in the Homes' contacts, the following sentence appears, "Von Braun is with us; the contact has been allowed." (Senkowski, ibid, Italian translation, p. 26).

I mean, even such a high profile personality as Wernher von Braun needed permission to make contact. Many years earlier, one of the voices recorded by Dr Konstantin Raudive stated "Kant does not have any importance here." (Raudive's *Breakthrough*, p. 30).

Again I emphasize that the concurrence of ITC messages received by different experimenters who did not know each other, who are in different parts of the world, in a time span of several decades, is a decisive argument in favour of the genuineness of the messages and that they are independent of the experimenters' minds. The common pattern that emerges from these remarkable similarities allows us to identify the next dimension as a separate structure, which resembles our world but has proper values, rules and peculiarities very unlike ours.

Chapter 6

THE NEXT WORLD

I was baffled the first time I heard a voice say right at the beginning of a DRV session "The other world has already responded!" This happened at the very moment I started speaking back to the voices. I did not know what to think and it worried me. What was this 'other world' they were now speaking of? It could not have been their world because they were not speaking to me but about me since the voice said "the other world has already responded" the very moment I started speaking back to the voices therefore, responding.

Clearly this time they were not answering my question because I had not asked any question, I had just greeted the communicators when I heard their voices. Sometimes when I ask who is speaking they reply, "We are from the other world!" But this time it had not happened this way. Thus, they must have been speaking of our own world, the earth! I was stunned because it was weird to hear our world be called "the other world", exactly the same expression we use when we speak about their world.

On another occasion, I heard a feminine voice distinctly say (apparently to somebody in her surroundings) "Be aware, I am speaking to the other world [ours]", obviously recommending him or her not to disturb the communication. How odd the whole situation seemed to me! Nevertheless, with the continuation of the DRV contacts, I got used to the communicators' use of the expression "the other world", meaning both theirs and ours.

A Pure World

Indeed, the communicators often use the same expression, "the other world", with different connotations. A good example is one extraordinarily long and clear recording, part of which is included in my CD and MP3 file, 'Electronic Voices' (example 21).[5] In it the anomalous voices repeatedly referred to their world as "the other world", while speaking with me. Most interesting is the fact that they also called their world a "pure world". They literally said (translation) "It is Rio do Tempo, it's from another pure world." "We are people from the other world, it's good!"

When I spoke back and asked "Is it you Rio do Tempo?" They repeated two or three times "It is Rio do Tempo," and continued with, "We are people from the other world; this one [earth] is not good for us." I thought they meant that they do not feel well in our world.

This time they identified themselves as "the other world" again and again, probably to render their identification unmistakable. I mean, they deliberately used an expression we understand easily because it is exactly the same one we use to speak about them. Perhaps they wanted to be sure that there would be no doubt about my recognition of them.

In addition, during this long conversation, the communicators referred to our world as "this one" or "this world". Does this mean that when the contact happened they were in our world as they often say they are? I suppose we could assume they were. But we also know that they can be in our world and in their world at the same time. This must be the reason why they often say "We are here with you" or "we are always with you" – information and expressions that have been received by almost every ITC operator in the world.

One of the many works of the well-known French theologian and electronic voices researcher, Father Dr François Brune, is a compilation of some of the most celebrated French automatic writing messages, the truthfulness of which, to my knowledge, has not been questioned. They were received by several members of the same family, throughout two generations, from the mid 1930s to 1980. Father Brune organized and assembled them in *Les Morts Nous Aiment* (Brune, 2009).

In this book, which I started reading only recently, I found a 1939 message from Jean Winter – one of the two deceased messengers who conveyed information to the family – which speaks about the purity that Rio do Tempo have so clearly avowed. It says (translation):

---

[5] http://www.itcjournal.org/?product=electronic-voices-cd-in-mp3-format

I continue a work that nothing stops in the middle of the happiness of no longer having to walk side by side with falsehood; of living in a vessel of clarity. In these planes in which I am side by side with pure souls only, you can imagine the wonder of having thought replace speech. If he reads in me, if I read in him, where could we place any lie whatsoever. All this to make you well understand – since on this plane impure souls cannot be found – that I continue to float, to move where I must be, with a sensation of ineffable joy. (Brune, ibid p. 162).

The Beauties of the Next World

The first time my communicators replied to my queries about their world, a beautiful masculine voice unmistakably answered my question of "Rio do Tempo, how is your world?", by saying "A world very similar to yours". This assertion is found in almost every report on the contacts with the next dimension, also by means other than ITC. I must admit that it is very difficult for me to envisage a world in another dimension very similar to our world, but this is what the communicators reiterate. Nevertheless, the similarity is obviously limited to the physical aspects of the worlds because our communicators also inform that, from the point of view of values, both worlds are completely different.

Carlos de Almeida, my beloved and first DRV communicator, whom I will mention often, once used a beautiful expression to describe his world. At the end of a rather long DRV communication, he said "Isto aqui tem muito serviço, é o portão da luz, é bonito aqui" ("There is a lot of work here; it is the gateway to the light, it is beautiful here!").

Along the same lines, my communicators have spoken of beautiful flowers and other wonders in their new world. When, many years ago, I asked "What is in your world?" my interlocutor replied "Our world, Anabela, has everything!" (literal translation). And to my insistent questioning "But how is your world?" they responded merrily on a couple of occasions "It's good!"

I believe the communicators themselves may realize the difficulties involved in trying to convey to us ideas about their world. For instance, my communicators often describe their lives – usually my family members' and my dogs' living conditions – using expressions such as: "Bela [my petname] we are in heaven!" or "We live in heaven!" and so on.

One of the abandoned dogs I adopted, little "Rio", died a few years ago. On the 9th September 2012, exactly one month after his passing, I asked Rio do Tempo about him: Rio do Tempo how is Rio? The masculine voice (I recall that the voice had identified itself as my father's) immediately replied: "O Rio está no céu!" (Rio is in heaven!).

I very much doubt any religious connotation was attached to the word 'céu' (heaven) because none of my family members were catholic or professed any other religion or creed. Overall, they were all agnostic and the concept of 'heaven', as understood by our western religions, played no role in their mental universe; perhaps just a cultural, symbolical one. And I think that the use of the word 'heaven' is a way of expressing their ecstasy at, and enjoyment of, their new life conditions. They could use it symbolically as we so often do. Together with the expression "we are happy", "we are in heaven" is a recurrent statement in their communications, and I believe that it could be taken as a way of describing their state of mind in their new surroundings.

On the same page (162) of François Brune's book, from which I quoted above, Jean Winter again says, "We are happy, this is what we deem most important to let you know; we teach you divine evolution but the exact scale of this evolution, you cannot entirely know it". The similarity to what ITC communicators have told us many years later (the French message is from 1940) needs no further comment.

Sceptics will almost certainly consider that expressions like the many I have recorded, "We are in heaven", "We are happy", etc. are trivial. I totally disagree and I am sure any well-intentioned person will concur. What indeed could be more important for us than knowing that those we think dead are alive and happy? What is trivial about this?

Another proof of our dear deceased ones' delight at their new world was conveyed by a masculine voice, apparently my father's, a few years ago. I had asked my father if the hardships he had gone through during his life on the earth were worth it in view of his new life. The masculine voice replied "Valeu tudo a pena!" (It was all worth it!). And in 1941, in France, Jean Winter said "I would so much like to give you, even for a few seconds, a vision of what our state is for us. You would be so dazzled that nothing from the earth would count for you any longer. And you could even suffer great pain almost without noticing." (Brune, ibid 2009).

The Auroras

I am a great lover of beautiful skies and the effects of light on them. So, one day, during one of my attempts to communicate telepathically with Rio do Tempo (a totally subjective act, the outcome of which I cannot avow to be correct as I have explained earlier), I chatted mentally with my communicators and said "The sky is beautiful today. Do you also have beautiful skies in your world?" Their unexpected reply, also mentally perceived, was "Skies always reflect the divine magnificence; we have the auroras!" I was surprised because such an idea had never crossed my mind and I have never seen an aurora. But, as usual, I did not take in the information to the letter. Unlike the recorded electronic voices, these are contacts and information that I cannot confirm and, thus, I just let them rest in my heart.

Notwithstanding the fact that, at the beginning of my telepathic contacts with Rio do Tempo, my communicators informed me of several desirable conditions to improve the communications and those were later confirmed by the results. But these little chats, which I love to have with them, are of a different nature; they are something I cherish but would never put forward as proof of anything.

Hence, I was delighted when, very recently, I found in François Brune's *Les Morts Nous Aiment* the following description conveyed by the deceased Jean Winter through automatic writing in 1940:

There are all the planes and all the colours; I have already told you. Blue encircles me, green is higher but for moments everything mingles in a harmony which gives the impression of blue but which is absolutely not the blue that you can think of. The green, the blue, even the red, even the orange form a set which renders blue dominant... No, I don't mean that. Imagine a succession of colours; this is what I mean by saying above: Blue, Orange, Red, Violet, Green. A rainbow which, when it disappears, mingles all the colours. Then the blue seems to predominate but on another moment it may be the green... beautiful is not enough. Dazzling, rather ... I see less and less of the earth, the sky is so beautiful, my dearest little mommy. (Brune, 2009, pp. 94-95).

There are Many Worlds

I have described, above, some of the expressions of great joy and gratitude, which my communicators have used to speak about their world; the bliss for being in such a magnificent place is manifest whenever they can speak about their life. This does not happen often, though, and I believe there is a reason for it. I will return to this aspect of the communications later. In any case, we should not forget that my Rio do Tempo partners (and other ITC communicators) state that "there are many worlds" corresponding to the different levels of consciousness of the beings that live in them. Therefore, I can convey to my readers only the portrait of the level of life that my own communicators convey to me. There may be many others.

Walking in the beautiful park, Tête d'Or in Lyon, France, where I lived for five years, I once saw a pigeon, among the many that wandered in the park, with both legs tied with a strong nylon thread. It could not walk; it had to jump from place to place, always reaching the last breadcrumb too late to catch it; the other pigeons had already eaten everything. I am a great lover and admirer of animals and the plight of this little bird that looked thin and astonished at its own incapacity highly disturbed me. I could not sleep properly all night. The evilness I had witnessed hurt me awfully. How could someone do such a thing to a poor, defenceless little bird? I could not find an answer. Thus, on the first opportunity I asked my communicators: Rio do Tempo, do people like the person who did this horrible thing to the little pigeon live in your world when they end their lives in our world? Their DRV reply simply said: "No, they live around Rio do Tempo [world]".

The Concept of 'Place' in the Next World

I have used the word 'place' in speaking about the next world and I am aware that it may be questioned because the concept of place is intimately connected to our three-dimensional world. We have no way of knowing what a place might be in the scope of another dimension. Nevertheless, we need to use concepts we know; there is no other way. For us it is 'their place'. We lack models to describe what appear to us to be non-local situations as is the case of the electronic voices' dimension.

Interestingly, Carlos de Almeida himself has explicitly used the word 'place' while talking with me. This happened right at the beginning of my DRV contacts when insistently I asked if he was speaking from Rio do Tempo Station, something I used to do as frequently as I could. Naturally a confirmation of the source of the communications is always very important. His very clear and loud reply confirmed "Yes, the place is, is here!" On this occasion he used two concepts related to space i.e., 'place' and 'here'.

I should add that such a clear, unmistakable direct confirmation that the DRV I was receiving originated at Rio do Tempo Station made me very happy. Later on there were innumerable others but, at the time, everything was new and the idea of a station in another world used to make me very nervous. As a matter of fact, I must confess that still I cannot fully assume the reality of these communications and the wonderment they cause me.

Also recently, I found a paragraph in John Fuller's book on the Spiricom, *The Ghost of 29 Megacycles*, which expresses exactly what I wish to convey to my readers. It refers to a conversation William O'Neil had with the apparition of Doc Nick. Apparently William O'Neil was clairvoyant and clairaudient and, before he started receiving proper electronic voices, he reported many mediumistic contacts to George Meek about the development of the Spiricom work.

In this instance, O'Neil asked Doc Nick what his world was like and the apparition responded like this:

> For now, Bill, let's just say it's pretty much the same as where you are. But much, much more, too. But since you can't believe completely what's happening, even at this very moment, with me here and you there – you know what I'm talking about. I'm just afraid you'd – no, not pass out, that's not what I mean – lose your mind or something like that (p. 133).

The most remarkable aspects of this message are: firstly, that it matches fully what Rio do Tempo told me many years later about the next world; and secondly, that the recipient cannot absorb fully the reality of his or her own contacts. Such is the power of our prejudices and mental patterns.

The sentence "you can't believe completely what's happening, even at this very moment, with me here and you there..." struck me in particular because that is exactly how I feel normally. However, when I am listening directly to the voices while they are coming from the radio, they sound not only completely true but also, strangely, very normal.

They are so strong and compelling that they convey an intense feeling of closeness and reassuring warmth. It is similar to what we feel when we return home to our beloved ones after a very long stay abroad – but much more moving and powerful. After all, we thought they were lost forever! The revelation of what undoubtedly appears to be the continuation of life after physical death has no parallel in any other emotion I have experienced or can think of.

Also, in my case, as I have explained elsewhere, I had not had any contact with the world of unexplained phenomena previous to the ITC voices I receive. Naturally, this circumstance plays an important role in my reactions.

The communicators have mentioned that they live in space, albeit another space, as we will see later. In any case, since they confirm that they also have a body, they must necessarily live in *a* space; consequently, the use of expressions such as 'place' and 'here' as we just saw.

But Where is this New World?

I have already touched on the puzzling issue of 'another dimension' and suggested that the subject of location was problematic because we cannot think properly in terms of a 'place' outside our three-dimensional world. Nevertheless, at the beginning of my DRV contacts, when I could often ask questions and get replies from Carlos de Almeida, Filipe, Joan Colbert and others, some apparently unknown to me, I used to ask the question repeatedly – "Where is your world?" or "Where are you?" At the time, the issue of dimensions and all that it implies was not yet in my thoughts. I lived in permanent awe and the situation somehow rendered my intellect less inquisitive.

The reactions of my interlocutors to my questions about the location of their world were vague and obscure most of the times. I remember that the first time they replied to my specific query of "Where are you?", they said something, which was obviously a joke: "We are beyond the 'Tejo'!" (The Tejo [Tagus in English] is the big river that flows into the sea near Lisbon). I used to get really baffled and worried with this sort of reply. I discovered, later, that a sense of humour is a recurrent characteristic of our dear communicators. As a matter of fact they never show sadness, a bad mood or irritation. But they often give proof of ethically directed critical sense.

Interestingly, they also have a tendency to minimize our problems and unhappiness. I remember in the beginning, while speaking to Rio

do Tempo, that I used to think mournfully about my deceased beloved ones and cry. On a couple of occasions an unidentified voice advised "Don't pay attention to her complaints!" obviously addressing the
other voice that was speaking with me. Naturally, if we view the situation from their perspective, our complaints, mainly concerning bereavement and related difficulties, lose much impact and *raison d'être*.
They are perfectly aware of the transitory nature of our problems, no
matter how dramatic they may seem to us. Recently my communicators told me "In your world everything is very fast", something which
is undeniably true.

Going back to the subject of location, on one occasion, immediately
after my recurrent request of "Rio do Tempo where is your world?" an
imposing masculine voice, very different from the usual ones because
it was a grave, authoritarian voice, interrupted the flow of the conversation I was having with my unidentified communicator to warn loudly
"Not to that!"; obviously indicating that he or she should not respond
to my question. I should explain here that, occasionally, the electronic
voices cannot easily be identified by gender since, at times, they sound
a little robotic.

I became even more puzzled and rather nervous because somehow,
in my mind, an indication of the location of their world would confirm
the reality of that mysterious 'other world' which Rio do Tempo spoke
of. This shows how the concept of space influences our thought. As
should be expected, we cannot reason properly outside its scope. On
subsequent occasions, though, different voices, subtle and discreet,
replied more precisely to my insistent queries. One day when I insisted "Where are you?" somebody replied. "We are in an apex of space."
Then on another occasion they responded, "We have another space."

The most decisive and important information came through one
day, quite unexpectedly, when, at a loss with the kind of replies I was
getting, I once more tried to pierce the veil of mystery and asked "Rio
do Tempo, is your world in our universe?" This time a gentle voice replied softly "It's another universe." And this extraordinary information sounded not only very coherent and true to me, but was also a key
factor in making me halt the persistent questions, about the location
of their world, with which I had been bombarding my communicators
until then. I realized that there was not much I could understand if we
were dealing with another universe.

Chapter 7

THE ILLUSIVE NATURE OF
APPEARANCES

The deceased Friedrich Jürgenson is reported as transmitting through a computer text the following message (see below the image of the screen filmed by Adolf Homes with his video camera):

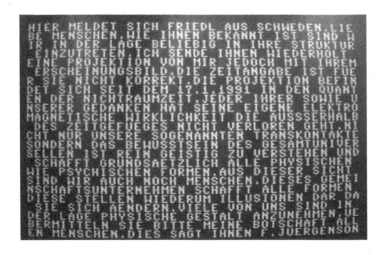

Translation of the German text above:

Here, Friedel from Sweden is making contact. Dear humans. As is known to you, we are in a position to enter into your structure at choice. I send you repeatedly a projection of myself but with your appearance [the appearance known to you]. The time indication [on the video-camera] is not correct for you. The projection is in the quanta of no space-time since 17.1.1991. Each [one] of your and of our thoughts has its own electromagnetic reality that does not get lost outside of the time structure. Not only our so-called transcontacts, but the consciousness of the universal whole (des Gesamtuniversellen) is to be understood [as] purely mental/spiritual and in principle creates all physical and psychical forms. From this point of view we, too, are still humans. This collective undertaking creates all forms. These, in their turn, represent illusions, because they change. Many of us are in a position to adopt [a] physical shape.

Please transmit my message to all men. This says to you F. Juergenson." (Senkowski, 1995; ITC Journal 39, 2010 pp. 35-61).

This fascinating computer text, one of many received by Adolf Homes, contains extremely interesting statements, which we will try to catch the sense of. Firstly, the elusive issue of appearance. It says: "I send you repeatedly a projection of myself but with your appearance" [the appearance known to us]. We could interpret this in many different ways, the first one being obviously the illusory nature of our physical form. Although we need not Zeitstrom's[6] (2) teachings to reach such conclusion – for we only need to observe carefully the changes in human and other animals' appearance in a life span – the message very clearly reflects the false nature of our physical form, of all physical forms. Also, when Jürgenson specifically mentions his appearance calling it "our" appearance, i.e. the shape of him that we know, this implies that he may have other appearances unknown to us. And this might include his new look in his new world.

Below is the image that appeared on Homes' TV screen simultaneously with the computer text in an adjacent room. (Note: the computer switched itself on without Homes' intervention);

---

[6] Zeitstrom is the original name in German of Timestream group.

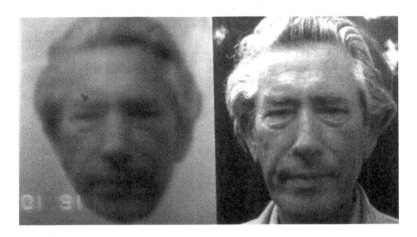

Left: the image which appeared on Homes TV screen.
Right: a lifetime photograph of Jürgenson for comparison.

The anomalous image is very similar to a late middle-age Jürgenson. This was the appearance he chose to show himself in (a projection of himself as he puts it). Because even in our physical world he had had other appearances as we all do. He chose this one, resembling his physical image almost at the end of his earthly life, perhaps because it was the freshest one in the memory of all who knew him and, therefore, the easiest one to identify.

Carlos de Almeida, my main communicator when I started receiving the DRVs, unexpectedly said one day in the middle of his talk "... I am already free from illusion!" Some months later, he said that he was leaving Rio do Tempo world and going into another [more elevated] world (Cardoso ibid, 2010).

The deceased Frederic Myers, purportedly through the automatic writing of Geraldine Cummins (Cummins 1932, 2012), informs extensively about the plane of illusion in the next world. In his book *Life Beyond Death* (2009), David Fontana also refers to it at length:

Therefore, this is the first feature of appearance: its changeability. Something that is transitory, ever-changing, is illusive because it cannot be truly real. It never reaches the state of being; it stays in the state of 'giving the impression of being', 'looking like' (something), if I can put it this way.

And, inevitably, the Sanskrit term 'Maya' in its widespread meaning of illusion, of chimera, comes to mind when we speak of appearance.

Heinrich Zimmer (1962), the brilliant Hindulogist, says about Maya:

The Hindu mind associates such ideas as transitory, ever-changing, elusive, ever-returning with 'unreality' and conversely, imperishable, changeless, steadfast, and eternal, with 'reality'.

As long as the experiences and sensations that stream through the consciousness of an individual remain untouched by any widening, devaluating vision, the perishable creatures that appear and vanish in the unending cycle of life (samsara, the round of rebirth) are regarded by him as utterly real. But the moment their fleeting character is discerned, they come to seem almost unreal – an illusion or mirage, a deception of the senses, the dubious figment of a too restricted, ego-centered consciousness. When understood and experienced in this manner, the world is Maya-Maya, 'of the stuff of Maya. Maya is 'art': that by which an artefact, an appearance, is produced.

The sentence "... But the moment their fleeting character is discerned, they [the perishable creatures] come to seem almost unreal ..." brought to my mind the sensation I have often experienced in regards to death – it cannot be true! This feeling of unreality has been so deep and intense that it even made me deny the event of death, as it happened when my dog Surya passed away.

The remembrance in my mind is that of a gloomy and rainy morning but I could not be sure because I was in a state of mind of great misery; thus, it could also have been a glorious sunny morning. One of the construction workers in my property at the time (the house was being repaired) told me that somebody in the nearby village had told him Surya had died and he asked me if it was true. Spontaneously I replied that no, of course it was not true! I said it so suddenly and could not understand why I had said it but I felt that I could not say anything else. A really strange feeling!

Back to F. Jürgenson's Computer Text

The Jürgenson text states:

... the consciousness of the universal whole (des Gesamtuniversellen) is to be understood [as] purely mental/spiritual and in principle creates all physical and psychical forms. And I believe it is legitimate to ask what the consciousness of the universal whole is. First of all, what is this universal whole? Our universe? Is it all that exists in this, and other, universes unknown to us? Or is it what we call God?

Furthermore, a fascinating message from Henri Sainte-Claire Deville received in Luxembourg, which we will explore further in a subsequent chapter, says at a certain point:

> ... The void dreams the universe, but the void is unconscious. Universe has consciousness and it can control the voice ...", and he goes on: "I repeat: the universe is dreamt by the void. It is varied out of grains, grains of virtual existence, grains called selectons ...

And we notice that it says practically the same as Jürgenson in the Homes' message because we can compare the creative "purely mental consciousness of the universal whole" to Deville's "universe dreamt by the void.... varied out of grains of virtual existence. ... " In both messages consciousness creates all forms, all illusions.

In addition the DRV communicator who identified himself as Filipe from Rio do Tempo Station declared at my house (excerpt of a long DRV message): "...the unconsciousness of God covers all ..." (literal translation). Next day when I spoke with Rio do Tempo, I remarked that I thought God was total consciousness and immediately a feminine voice replied "So did I, only God knows!"

There appears to be a parallel between Sainte-Claire Deville's "void" and Filipe's "unconsciousness of God". The void, which "is unconscious", dreams and in so doing, creates an illusion, our universe, which has consciousness. In Filipe's message the "unconsciousness of God covers all". Again, nothingness, the void, embraces all that exists, i.e. consciousness. A remarkable similarity expressed in different terms. We should remember, however, that the modern concept of void (fluctuating field/s of virtually infinite probabilities/possibilities) has nothing to do with the ancient concept of void, vacuum, emptiness.

In Deville's DRV in Luxembourg, Jürgenson's computer text at Adolf Homes' and Filipe's DRV message at my house, our universe is presented as a virtual creation and not as a true, permanent reality. An idea in the fashion of the Vedic concept of Maya, as we saw earlier; an illusion where things (everything) appear, indubitably, to exist but, in truth, they do not. They are shapes and, thus, illusions. Things that change cannot truly exist because being implies permanence, eternalness, which is the opposite of transiency. We could also call to our discussion quantum physics and the illusory nature of matter, and we would be speaking of the same thing. But I have no expertise in the field; I am only a layperson extremely interested in these connections which, unfortunately, I cannot pursue. Our discussion would need quantum physicists to get involved and, sadly, they do not appear to be interested.

Going back to the Homes' message, we find that Friedrich Jürgenson's computer text contains an amazing statement: "... Each [one] of your and of our thoughts has its own electromagnetic reality that does not get lost outside of the time structure ...". Although modern science has not yet recognized the permanent reality, or even the electromagnetic nature of thoughts, it seems that it is starting to investigate this field. But Jürgenson puts it clearly in a text received over twenty years ago, on October 13, 1994.

From his side, during the same contact, my beloved communicator Filipe used a wonderful expression, which I took up as the motto for the ITC Journal: "Pense sempre em nosso mundo; quem pensa no nosso mundo as distâncias reduz." (Always think of our world; whoever thinks of our world reduces the distances). This marvellous advice seems to confirm Jürgenson's statement about thoughts not being lost outside of the time structure. Furthermore, when Filipe said this in March 1998, I knew nothing of the computer text received by Adolf Homes. Although the message is published in Dr Senkowski's book, I only knew about these extraordinary communications rather recently, directly from him when he gave me the book. And I started reading the Italian version, only when I started writing this book, a couple of years ago.

Even more recently, just a few months ago, I was thrilled to discover in François Brune's book a message received in 1959 from the deceased Gérald de Dampierre in reply to a question from his living friend Philippe:

> ... But you also think of those whom you have known and who are departed and with them this chain is formed, of which I have already told you; and this chain has repercussions on the earth and on us because it spreads through the thoughts of each other to those who are with us and to those who are still on the earth; this is the reason why all, and you [also] must be attentive and always be welcoming and good. (ibid, p.227).

What could be more similar to "always think of our world"? The amazing intricacies of ITC messages are another characteristic that renders these incredible communications truly fascinating.

Chapter 8

THE BODY

Its Nature and Shape in the Next World

Many people think that if survival is true we survive in ethereal form without a body because we left it on the earth. According to the communicators, nothing is further from the truth. They say "We also have a body. It is a more beautiful, much more flexible body than yours." And it seems that beautiful body also feels sensations just like ours but in a more refined and developed way.

When we speak of a body in the context of the next dimension, we are speaking of, to us, an invisible body but still a body. My communicators have told me that their body is made of a kind of electricity, and this could be the clue to understanding interesting aspects of a number of other phenomena related to survival, namely apparitions and their fugacity. Also, the great number of electrical occurrences associated with the deceased seems to be relevant (See Puhle, Annekatrin 2014 *Light Changes* and Wright, Sylvia H., 1998 and 2002 (ch 9).

At the beginning of my DRV contacts and, to a certain extent, even today, lots of unexplained electrical incidents happened in my house. In addition, a highly penetrating direct radio voice, which sounded very much like Carlos de Almeida's customary voice, yelled one evening loudly and clearly, during a DRV contact, "Oh Pierre liga o circuito pos-to aí" ("Oh Pierre connect the circuit put there") "É um sonho meu!" ("It's a dream of mine!"). "Vocês vejam lá o circuito e as instalações de luz ..." ("So you check the circuit there and the light installations") and he carried on with other comments (See CD Electronic Voices, exam-ple 6 'VOU À ALMA'). The voice was so loud that I have to lower the volume of the recording whenever I play it at a conference.

In my book *Electronic Voices* I describe what I felt as a kind of elec-trical current passed through my hand, which I had resting on my dog Michi's chest the moment she died. It felt like an electrical discharge but much, much finer and more vibrant. It did not hurt at all. It was more like a pleasant energetic feeling, were it not for the circumstances.

In his *Les Morts Nous Aiment* (p.145) François Brune cites a mes-sage received by the daughter of the French EVP pioneer Monique Si-monet about the body in the next world. Stéphane, a deceased young friend of the family, said to Muriel, Simonet's daughter, "You cannot truly imagine my body. It is different from Axel's ... [Muriel's deceased son]. Axel's body is still rather similar to what it was on earth: my body is extremely brilliant, totally irradiating; it is similar to a sort of accu-mulation of rays... you would not be able to distinguish my eyes, my face... what I am, is beyond that" (Simonet, 1991).

The Influence of Electricity and Atmospheric Conditions

Nobody put it better than two of the very first pioneers in Instru-mental Transcommunication, Dr J. L. Matla and Dr G. J. Zaalbert van Zelst, from Holland, both trained physicists who initiated their re-search in 1904. Scott Rogo and Raymond Bayless in their remarkable book *Phone Calls from the Dead* report extensively on the Dutch sci-entists' highly interesting and successful experiments, which involved the design and setting up of new devices, basically electrical in nature, intended to attempt the communication with the deceased. And I quote from the above mentioned work:

> One of Matla's most intriguing discoveries was that atmospheric conditions had a noticeable effect on [their] machine. Humid and rainy weather seemed to inhibit good results while the best communications were received during the drier seasons.

This information was corroborated by one of our own ITC communicators during the controlled experiments carried out in the School of Engineering's Acoustics Laboratory at Vigo University, in Spain (See *NeuroQuantology*, 2012). During one experiment, which used the reversed speech of operators and participants as acoustic background, one of the Portuguese operators, Maria dos Anjos Antunes, asked the invisible interlocutors if the atmospheric conditions had influence on the contacts. The reply by a masculine voice clearly said "Much influence." Unfortunately, this voice and pertinent information were not quoted in the report I published in *NeuroQuantology* because a great number of other louder voices were recorded during this particular experiment. Thus, finding the quality of the voice less striking than the other ones, I did not mention it. I regret it now because, although the voice was soft, the information it conveyed was relevant, mainly in view of other ITC experimenters' observations, which affirm the same thing. However, I must confess that I have received voices – DRV and EVP – in practically all kinds of atmospheric conditions.

But extremely interesting is also the fact that the French automatic writing messages that I have been citing, say practically the same thing! And I translate from page 29:

Forgive me for the bad communication and writing. I wanted to tell you so many things and I was above all busy with your physical condition. Stormy weather, very little favourable to the communications. Do not believe that the atmospheric disturbance does not bother us – it stops the vibrations, or, if you prefer, upsets them. To move down to you becomes almost impossible." (Jean Winter to his mother).

Conversely, one of Adolf Homes' communications states that: "these contacts are not weather dependent" (Senkowski, German original, p. 47. 1999).

We should not immediately point at discrepancies in the information above. First of all, our Rio do Tempo communicators have said that atmospheric conditions influence the contacts, not that the contacts are dependent on the weather conditions. I have received DRV contacts during all kinds of weather conditions with the exception of heavy electrical storms when my communicators have expressly indicated that the radios must be turned off. But, very recently, during a mild electrical storm, I also received a short piece of the DRV. Very surprised, I asked my communicators how had they been able to speak during a thunderstorm and a soft feminine voice remarked: "It is more difficult". Furthermore, we do not know which kind and which level of contacts Homes' communicators referred to. Allegedly Homes' communicators were entities of high ranking, possibly higher beings of non-human origin, and this circumstance could be important.

Dr Matla also discovered that certain types of electrical currents channelled through the device helped generate stronger results. Actually he came to the conclusion that "the very element of our personality that survives death is partially electrical in nature and has an affinity for manipulating electrical energy" (Scott Rogo and Bayless, 1979).

The Body Again

When my communicators told me that they also have a body, a more beautiful, more flexible body than our bodies in this dimension, I asked what feelings they experienced through that body. And it seems that their subtler body also experiences sensations similar to the ones we experience in this world including the ones associated with sex, among others.

Although I perceived this information telepathically from Rio do Tempo, I found the same topic explicitly mentioned in the Luxembourg report:

> ... Friendships and partnerships continue to be nourished. Sexuality is not rejected, being part of the human nature, provided both partners harmonize and wish it. Animals too, continue to live in the third level after their bodily death. They lack nothing and are being cared for by animal-loving humans. We eat and drink like you do. Our nourishment is "synthetic", i.e. we materialize earthly food, so to speak ...

Specifically, about the body, communications received via the Burton Bridge in Luxembourg, which reportedly were of extreme clarity, stated that:

> We have a body like yours. It consists of finer matter and faster vibration than in your dense, coarse material world. There is no sickness here...
> (Locher and Harsch, 1989).

In the course of my former DRVs when the contacts were pouring almost daily and I could have not only a coherent dialogue with my partners, but also listen to many conversations between them, I record-ed several voices (not always the same ones) say to each other "Let's go out and have a cup of coffee," together with other comments of simi-lar nature. I must admit that this type of conversation topics, which I could hear directly and which I recorded, used not only to flabbergast me but also to make me very nervous. At that time, I found it unthink-able that things like going out for a cup of coffee could take place in the next world, in another dimension. I see now that although I have always considered myself an open-minded person, capable of accept-ing 'impossible' things, my attitude was certainly the result of subcon-scious prejudices, which I did not know existed in my mind.

Back in the eighteenth century, Swedenborg, the great Swedish mystic and scientist, had already passed on information about some of the next world's features based on his own experiences. "The spiritual world", he wrote, "in external appearance is altogether similar to the natural world. Man, when he is loosed from the body, appears as a man in the world. He has senses, touch, smell, hearing, sight, far more exquisite than in the world . . . for life after death is a continuation of life in the world."

In the French messages assembled by François Brune in *Les Morts Nous Aiment*, we find many references of the use of senses similar to our own. For example, says Gerald de Dampierre in 1957:

> We have, take good note, the same perceptions that we have on the earth, almost exactly the same. I have told you that I could touch you if I wanted but that I had no wish to do that. We are extremely close, much closer than you can ever be aware of.

In my studio during an extremely noisy session of the DRV, a voice can be heard in the recording saying clearly and loudly "Oh, I cannot stand this noise!"

Indeed, the radios were making unbearable noise that evening. On other occasions the voices remarked "It seems that it is going to rain," "It is cold!" and so on. There are also, of course, their many comments related to vision. The communicators are aware of everything in my studio and at my house, e.g. the colour of my little cat who had stayed in the recording room, a new device in my studio, sand in my feet, when I had just arrived from the beach going directly to the studio etc.

We may now compare those remarks I recorded to some of Dr Rau-dive's voices of the end of the 1960s: "It smells the rain here"; "Great fog"; "It will rain"; Oh thunder!"; "West wind!"; "Kosta [Raudive's pet-name], warm"; "It is raining here", etc.

Is the striking resemblance between comments made by the anomalous electronic voices and recorded within a time span of fifty years, accidental? Or is it the result of a common pattern? I will let my readers decide but I consider that such strong coincidences are among the most impressive testimonies not only of the reality of the next dimension, but also of the common attributes that pertain to it and to the beings that live there.

Filipe's admirable DRV message that I have been introducing to my readers also included this sentence: "... and I feel a very English collie [at the time of the contact a collie dog was playing in my garden with the other dogs] ... I feel a little heather [there are lots of heather shrubs in the hills around my house]... and I feel another colour ... etc." Here, on the other hand, Filipe said "I feel" not "I see". When I read Father Brune's messages, I found a line that perhaps explains this. In reply to a question by his mother: Are there flowers where you are? The deceased Gérald de Dampierre replied: "Naturally there are. We are surrounded by them. There are [flowers] of all kinds, of all colours and you know that I loved them. Yes, indeed, I am filled with wonder to see them, to contemplate them and even to feel them! This surprises you but it's like that." Thus, apparently our communicators can see, hear and all the other senses just as we do, and simultaneously feel what they see, hear, etc. This is, of course, a big step beyond our senses.

One of the pieces of information received from the next world, which puzzled me most, was that their earthly bodies somehow also reach the next world. This was telepathically perceived by me and it possibly means that an ethereal double of our bodies in this dimension also passes into the next world. As I have repeated before, I am not knowledgeable of esoteric traditions and all they entail, such as the astral body, the double etc. But my assumption seems to be corroborated by one of the long anomalous computer texts received in Luxembourg from Dr Swejen Salter (Zeitstrom Station). I transcribe, below, an excerpt of that message and will continue with the transcription of the same message in another chapter.

... Some people or animals wake up here reborn, so to speak. This was the case with K. Others like the one you call Margret Mackes come to us as old people and turn young again after the regenerating sleep. Why there are such differences, we do not know. At the end of the growth or rejuvenation process people will be around 25 or 30 years old. Animals will be at an age of vitality and well-being at which they feel best since esthetical factors are not involved here. Damaged tissue or broken bones regenerate just like wounds heal in your world but much more perfect. Lost limbs will re-grow. The blind will see again and so on. The colour of your hair and skin cannot be changed and will be the same as during your Earth life. Here in the river world, beings arrive from all levels of life ...

And Filipe, my dear communicator, corroborated this. His long DRV talk also included the following passage "Rio do Tempo fora do contexto ... E sinto um collie bem inglês e não se preocu[pe] ... *es tão jovem como um perro destes!* ..... e sinto um pouco de urze. ..." (Literal translation: Rio do Tempo out of context .... And I feel a very English collie and do not worry, he is as young as any of these dogs! ... and I feel a little heather. ... ")

Although he does not say any name, only "he", Filipe could only be speaking of my dog Surya whose departure from my life had been the cause of deep grief and despair for me. Indeed, I was constantly anxious about him, missing him terribly. The deep pain had been, and still is, always with me. With the passing of time it has eased, of course, but not because of the time that went by; much more important has been Rio do Tempo's constant assurance that life continues. When Filipe said, "... he is as young as any of these dogs" he was obviously referring to the dogs playing in my garden at the time of the contact, Red, the collie, among them. Although they were abandoned dogs, they had recovered, becoming healthy and playful again.

I must emphasize that, in spite of Surya's appalling health condition when he died (due to visceral leishmaniasis and kidney failure), Filipe said, "he is as young as any of these dogs!" and his remark fully matches the information received in Luxembourg about the rejuvenation of animals. This totally unexpected, exceptional message contains other highly interesting statements. It has made me happy since then.

Chapter 9

TIME, SPACE AND THE
NATURE OF LIFE

Time and Space

ITC communicators often mention the concept of "Time". They have
told me "You are in time, we are outside time", and have repeated similar statements on different occasions. But we cannot consider a world
without time. In our world, time means change in whatever way, per-
ceptible or imperceptible. What then is a world outside of time? I believe we cannot speculate much of value on this topic because we have
no reference point to guide us. But we will analyse what the communicators have said and try to reach some understanding, albeit limited
by our current human condition.

Conversely, to their use of the expression "the other world", as we
discussed in a previous chapter, when the communicators use the
word "space" it normally applies to our planet. Rio do Tempo voices
have merrily announced at the beginning of a number of contacts "We
are already in space", "We have entered space" and so on. Occasionally
they will also say "We are on the earth!" A voice, which identified itself
as my grandmother's, once told me "It is your grandmother speaking
from space!" And other members of my family, as well as unidentified communicators, have reiterated on numerous occasions "We are

speaking to you [me] from space!" The event seems to be cheerfully celebrated; the voices that announce the feat sometimes use a singing tone, they sound merry and lively perhaps because it means a difficult achievement. On many occasions the voices that announced "We are in space", or "We have entered space", "We are already in space" etc. did it in such a way that they conveyed an unmistakable feeling of joy and celebration. Interestingly and unexpectedly, I have found similar statements about "space" in Father Brune's compilation of the French automatic writing messages that I have been citing.

It seems that space-time, i.e. our world, is very important for our development. When I asked Rio do Tempo what the most important factor for (spiritual) growth was, they responded "It is time and it is space". This leads me to believe that life on the earth – together with the hardships, the suffering and the difficulties all living things must face in our world – decisively contributes to growth, to the expansion of consciousness that Rio do Tempo and other ITC communicators avow is the essential goal of life. Also, when I asked Rio do Tempo what the development process for non-human animals was, they replied that for them growth was achieved "through the hardships of the Natural Law". Similar statements were repeated in Luxembourg and at Adolf Homes' in Germany.

A Language Clarification

The use of expressions such as growth and spiritual development can, unfortunately, be found in the scope of New Age ideals. I dislike profoundly the popular and, above all, the commercialized version of this movement, which, in my opinion, has contributed greatly to trivializing truly transcendental and spiritual aspirations. The New Age followers seem to dwell on gurus, incense, false yoga and agreeable soft music. They remind me of the hippy movement of the sixties with their flowers and slogans, "make love not war", but emptier than the latter.

Nevertheless, although I do not adhere to the New Age terminology, I must use some of it, particularly the term spiritual growth, to convey to my readers the ideas I want to share with them. But even if I sometimes use the same words the New Age people have got hold of, I use them in a different sense. I will offer a few prosaic examples of what I would like to clarify. When, for instance, I speak of eating habits, I will value the fact of not eating animals out of respect for them instead of doing it for the sake of one's own health. As a matter of fact, I am unable to understand how a person who is not concerned with the welfare of our companions in this planet - animals, other humans, plants and the whole of Nature - can be 'spiritual'.

Furthermore, I do value the work done for others – independently of their gender, species or value – much more than beautiful moonlight rituals around a fire on the beach, listening to soft esoteric music and so on, so much the liking of New Age adepts. For instance, is not the wolf's desperate, exhausting chase for food in his territory, now depleted and abused by humans, nobler and more spiritual than a human celebration of the Summer solstice at dawn with a beef sandwich in one hand and a coca-cola in another? An act of veneration for supposed ancient Gods but without giving a thought to what a beef sandwich and a coca-cola represent? I suppose it all lies in the concept of spiritual which, for me, is an all-embracing notion that involves ethics, sacrifice and self-denial when needed, hardship, and, above all, compliance with the Natural Law.

These are only examples, which I deliberately wanted to be banal. Many more could be put forward but I hope they are enough to give my readers an idea of what I mean when I speak of the concepts misused in New Age terminology. When I employ such terms they will carry a different meaning. I understand that this might cause some confusion but I have no other way because there is no alternative terminology.

Back to the Concept of Time

We go back to the issue of time. Rio do Tempo voices have told me "We [they] are from another dimension; we are from beyond time." (Example 19, chant 4 of my CD.) And in Luxembourg, communicators from Timestream and Lifeline (a Station in the next world in cooperation with Timestream) informed similarly about time.

The French chemist Sainte-Claire Deville, whom we met in previous chapters, also refers to time in direct connection to the grains of virtual existence, which form our universe, and offers a very interesting explanation. With Prof. Ernst Senskowski's kind permission, I transcribe below from his book *Transkommunikation* (1995), what I consider to be one of the most fascinating texts in ITC literature.

In the presence of seven persons (B.W., J.P.S., Meek, Resch, Senkowski), Henry Sainte Claire Deville made contact on May 2nd, 1987, 8 p.m., as the speaker of transgroup LIFELINE (MTC partner of American METASCIENCE). He spoke in English with conspicuous French accent, directly via the loudspeaker of a USW receiver of the ESB within the 90 MHz range; intelligibility 100%. Investigations showed that drop-in communicator Deville, unknown to all those present, had been an excellent French chemist of the 19th century who, among others, was the first to study the properties of crystalline silicon. The year 1881, as that of his passing is correct.

My name is Henry Sainte Claire Deville. I left your world in 1881, and I am speaking to you in my name and in the name of our staff from LIFELINE, the scientists. Your project as well as [those] from LIFELINE and from TIMESTREAM is to set fire to minds, to set fire to minds in your world, and in that moment to try to master time. I can give you a few explanations.

The void dreams the universe, but the void is unconscious. Universe has consciousness and it can control the voice. A strong force, the inertia of normality, reigns in the universe. So the universe always chooses the same state as before; it sustains itself, it limits itself. I repeat: the universe is dreamt by the void. It is varied out of grains, grains of virtual existence, grains called selectons. Selectons are really tiny dots consisting of a circle rolled up compactly. Forever they roll back into the void; forever other bits of void roll back to replace them exactly. All these selectons rolled up compactly in the same direction, thus time flows in one direction in the universe. In our space selectons are not rolled up, so there in the Never-Ever all time is one and timeless.

Notwithstanding our previous analysis, this complex and mind-boggling description never ceases to puzzle me and I invite my readers to go on pondering over its content.

To start with Deville announced "Your project [the experimenters' task] as well as [those] from LIFELINE and from TIMESTREAM is to set fire to minds, to set fire to minds in your world ..."

We can certainly interpret the sentence "set fire to minds in your [our] world" as symbolic of the action needed to achieve a paradigm shift, and the subsequent expansion of consciousness it implies, urged by the communicators on many occasions, as we just saw. A paradigm shift is the major reason for setting fire to minds.

Other ITC messages have advocated the same attitude; we find a very elucidative example in the conversation that the deceased Dr Raudive had with a lady called Aline Piget in the first anomalous telephone call received in France. I quote the last paragraph of a paper by the French researcher Pierre Théry published in *ITC Journal* 2, 2000, pp. 42-43:

> ... I would like you to know, dear Aline, that the object of an earthly life is not just the goodness. The object is to be conscious. Some of your friends consider it just a matter of fashion – a phenomenon of society – when they speak of the results of modern ITC. They are wrong, as you know very well ... (the voice blurs) ... A long time ago ... (the voice vanishes completely).

> The statement – the object [of a life on the earth] is to be conscious – speaks for itself. Somebody from Rio do Tempo, using typical ITC language, simultaneously metaphoric and brief, speaks of the necessary expansion of human consciousness: "Falamos ao mundo, em todos os lugares, a abertura do caminho!" (We speak to the world, everywhere, the opening of the path!).

More of Adolf Homes' Messages

I have been extensively quoting the German experimenter Adolf Homes and the extraordinary information he received from high entities, mostly in the form of computer texts; one of those messages said the following on our topic:

> In many worlds, time and stability are illusory. All forms represent illusions because they are in a modification phase. Illusion is, therefore, all that is transitory. The composition of the information is the ultimate illusion. Body and mind [reason, intellect] are illusory. Space and time are illusions. The illusion of your time is to be attached to other illusions. You live in a space of illusion that we call time ... ('Transkommunikation', German original, p. 39. 1999).

One of the most fascinating lessons at Adolf Homes', and one which extraordinarily appeals to me, is the description of information. It says:

Information is the reality. All that exists is composed of information. ... All entities are constituted by information; we are also information. Because information is what you understand by the word 'be'. ... Everything is in the flow of information. If you were to put information in connection with energy, we would partially agree to this, because both are fundamental elements that never finish. All are available at any time. In all information, no matter where it comes from, there is neither a beginning nor an end, because everything is flowing. ... In the worlds reign innumerable forms of information. The information concerning the original divinity has become extraneous to you. Only the primordial information contains the truth (ibid p. 40).

We notice that Homes' entities stated:

"the composition of the information is the ultimate illusion". The composition of the information is the illusion but the flow of information is the reality. A paradox – as frequently happens in ITC messages? I believe not. The secret resides in accepting an apparent paradox as something deeper than that we can reach with the mind – the intellect – which is illusory ...

Back to Deville's message. We notice that when the communicator says, "In our space selectons are not rolled up, so there in the Never-Ever all time is one and timeless", he confirms the existence of space in their world – a timeless world in another space.

But at Homes' a high entity declared "I am in a non-space, timeless level". Homes' transmessages speak of the "Multiverse", multiple universes of countless probabilities, in which can originate innumerable life forms. Nothing is definitely this or that; everything is this and that or that and this in an amazing combination of probabilities. According to the high entities in contact with Adolf Homes, all levels of existence correspond to, and are created by, consciousness in its different levels of development.

At my house, Rio do Tempo confirmed that there are many life levels in the afterlife matching the consciousness development of the beings that inhabit them. Years before in Luxembourg, the Technician affirmed, in reply to a question by the experimenters, "There are many

planes below me and many planes above me. All these are again separated into other planes". Another remarkable concurrence!

Let me add that we should not make the mistake of considering some
of these messages incoherent or contradictory. In my opinion they are
nothing of the sort. They only reflect the infinite probabilities of life
and its boundless features.

The Transcendental Nature of Life

I take great pleasure in starting this section with the excerpt of a
speech Vaclav Havel pronounced in Philadelphia, in 1994:

> In today's multicultural world, the truly reliable path to coexistence, to
> peaceful coexistence and creative cooperation, must start from what
> is at the root of all cultures and what lies infinitely deeper in human
> hearts and minds than political opinion, convictions, antipathies, or
> sympathies – it must be rooted in self-transcendence: Transcendence
> as a hand reached out to those close to us, to foreigners, to the
> human community, to all living creatures, to nature, to the universe.
> Transcendence as a deeply and joyously experienced need to be
> in harmony even with what we ourselves are not, what we do not
> understand, what seems distant from us in time and space, but with
> which we are nevertheless mysteriously linked because, together with
> us, all this constitutes a single world. Transcendence as the only real
> alternative to extinction.[7]

This is the thought of somebody who, at the time, was still alive
and among us and, by quoting it, I wish to emphasize that we can find
different levels of consciousness in our world, too; similarly, our communicators tell us we will find them in the continuation of life in other worlds. Expansion of consciousness seems to be the key to it all.

As we have seen, and will continue to see throughout the book, the
majority of Rio do Tempo's statements, as well as the information received by other reputable ITC operators, point to the transcendental
nature of existence in opposition to the materialistic, pragmatic and

---

[7]   Source: Vaclav Havel. The need for transcendence in the postmodern world.
The Futurist. 1995; 29(4): 46 ff. Available at: http://www.worldtrans.org/
whole/havelspeech.html.

self-oriented view adopted by our society and the majority of people. Carlos de Almeida once said about his world: "This is the world of the soul that bets somewhere else [has different principles]". Notice the use of the word 'bet' (literally translated) which belongs to colloquial Portuguese. As a matter of fact, ITC communicators, even when they convey high teachings, very rarely use formal language and never a pedantic one.

It was very gratifying for me to find that, from the point of view of the next world, spiritual progress is not connected to any religion or spiritual practices but rather to the respect for Nature and every life form as well as to the inner development of consciousness. The higher entity, whom we call the Technician, declared in Luxembourg that "the respect for each living being is part of the upcoming spiritual development of man". And he added, "in the future ITC should encompass human rights and the protection of animals and of nature" (Locher and Harsch, 1989).

I have thought along the same lines for many, many years, long before I knew ITC existed and certainly long before I started my ITC experimentation. I suppose I have thought this way since I was able to think for myself, free from the influence of family and social environment. I am aware that detractors will suggest that I unconsciously model the messages I receive to my thought patterns. Since this affirmation cannot be disproved or proven, I opine that the messages I receive do come from my transpartners (an expression used by Professor Ernst Senkowski to designate our dear communicators) and that we belong to the same Group-Soul. Therefore, and since the Group-Soul is assembled by affinities, we share common understanding and perhaps this enables me to receive messages of the above and similar contents easily because my brain does not reject them. In addition, messages saying practically the same have been received by other ITC operators whom I do not know and who have obtained their contacts long before I started receiving mine. And this is such a very important point that I never tire of calling it to my readers' attention.

The message about the survival of plants, for instance, would fall into the same category. The pertinent voice is clear, although softly spoken, and it can be understood by anybody with knowledge of the language. However, let us imagine for a moment that the ITC operator who receives this information is an anthropocentric, anthropomorphic thinker who, as suggested by Flammarion, believes that "the moon shines to illuminate romantic nights for humans in love". Would such a person perceive the message in the same way I did? Isn't it true that the human brain adapts the information it receives to the patterns it recognizes? If this is the case, as it seems it is, the message about the survival of plants might never be understood. The latter would exist in the same phonetic form but the recipient would not be able to comprehend it no matter how clear it was and, especially, if it were muffled.

In Luxembourg, the Technician advised "The inhabitants of the Earth must learn to change their thought pattern... some will recognize, through ITC, the inutility of their material likings and will turn to spiritual interests." (Locher and Harsch, ibid 1989)

Anomalous computer texts received by Adolf Homes say practically the same thing:

> In this reality [ours] the danger of self-annihilation exists. The physical end is not far away because the man of the earth has lost his own dignity and has forgotten his own task because you live in a world that you have largely contributed to create. Because of the annihilating atomic schizophrenia you declared to nature, and thereby to yourselves, a war that nobody will win. (Transcomunicazione, p. 127).

Then a little further on: "To treat all living beings responsibly is the task of humanity" (ibid p. 128).

From her side, Maggy Harsch comments in her book with Theo Locher about the Luxembourg contacts:

> For the moment let me say that if we want to help others through ITC, let us do it not only for people who have lost relatives but also for those who have suffered from long illness, for the lonely, for animals, for our suffering environment, for peace in the world, and specially for eliminating ignorance, so that the path to the Light becomes the highest goal. (Locher and Harsch, ibid 1989)

The striking similarity to Rio do Tempo's loud and clear statement, "Hi, we speak from the other level, humans need to know about the Light!", is clear.[8]

Rereading this particular message received by Adolf Homes, "In this reality [ours] the danger of self-annihilation exists. The physical end is not far away because the man of the earth has lost his own dignity and

---

[8]   See www.itcjournal.org.

has forgotten his own task, because you live in a world that you have largely contributed to create..." I could not avoid thinking of the dramatic situation our planet is currently facing due to human activities. A situation which could indeed result in annihilation.

The transcendence of life, as conveyed by our communicators, is opposed to the way we understand existence in our world. As a matter of fact, being so different in values (albeit not in appearance), the next world comes out more like the spiritual reverse of our world than the next step in life's evolution that it is meant to be. Naturally, when I speak of our world I am speaking of the world we presently live in, not of worlds past. But perhaps it has not always been like this. Maybe we have lost the connection to the source we once had. Maybe we have lost the capacity we once had of understanding life's ways. I do not know; it is just a possibility among the many probabilities available to life that our communicators describe.

Chapter 10

THE ROLE OF AFFINITIES AND THE GROUP-SOUL

Affinities seem to play an important role in the next world. We have touched on the subject in a previous chapter and I have discussed it in earlier publications (Cardoso, 2010, 2003). Indeed, the meaning and importance of the Group-Soul described in the mediumistic literature, e.g. the information received purportedly from the deceased Frederic Myers by Geraldine Cummins (Cummins, 2012), have been emphasized in my own contacts.

But as early as 1857, the concept was already proposed. In his *Le Livre des Esprits* Alan Kardec, based upon the information purportedly received from the deceased, stated: "Experience shows us that spirits of the same degree, of the same character, and animated by the same sentiments are united in groups and families; ..." "Let us remark again that spirits are attracted to each other by the similarity of their qualities and that they, thus, form sympathetic groups or families."

More than one hundred and thirty years later, one of Adolf Homes' computer messages guaranteed, "When you pass away the trans-entities to which you belong because of your soul will await you".

Years ago, at the beginning of my ITC work, I received a long and very loud DRV which, among other things, literally says "...and I go down to my group, I go to the soul!" (See 'Electronic Voices' CD). Furthermore,

I have received replies to my questions on who was speaking, which clearly avow: "Somos nós todos!" [literal translation: It's we all!] and "It's your father speaking all together", or "It's your father, it's all of us!" Also, on several occasions: "It's your mother, it's all of us!" uttered by a masculine voice! Although the characteristics of the voices are not the topic of this work, I would like to remind the reader that, as I wrote earlier, the electronic voices very seldom resemble the physical voice of the individual they are supposed to belong to. The voices are synthesized and, thus, the resemblance must be a trait extremely difficult to achieve (see Locher and Harsch, 1989).

On one occasion, suddenly, in the middle of a DRV conversation, a voice emphasized: (translation) "... they live in communion". I deduced that "they" were the group in the next world that speaks with me. Interestingly, a few years ago, when I was present at the Bacci Centre in Grosseto during one of his DRV sessions, a voice replied to the questions I had unexpectedly put to the communicators, in Portuguese, with a phrase, also in Portuguese, that recommended the same attitude to us, here on the earth. It said "... Live happily and with great dignity; live it in loyalty and in communion..." (see *ITC Journal* 25, 2006, pp. 27-28 for a full transcript of the DRV messages). Hence, it seems that the ability to live in communion is a valuable tool for growth and development, and it should be practised by us, here, in this world, too.

Unexpectedly, some weeks ago, I found the exact expression my communicators use so frequently – "Nós todos" (We all) – in Father François Brune's book that we have been looking at. This time in French, "Nous tous", appears several times in the remarkable collection of mediumistic messages obtained by several members of the same family by the middle of the 20th century. One of such messages, received via automatic writing by the mother of the deceased Gérald de Dampierre, says at a certain point (translation):

> ... go on your trip without fearing and offer all who surround you a serene and joyful face. That will make me still happier. And we all ("nous tous"), also. You do not yet know the entire incredible meeting of all loving hearts, family and others that assembles here and will join me when you will all come and we will finally meet again (Brune, ibid p. 106).

Not only the sentence, one among many in this collection of mediumistic messages saying virtually the same thing, fully supports

the concept of the Group-Soul, but the phrase "nous tous" particularly struck me because my Rio do Tempo communicators have uttered exactly the same words in their contacts with me. The family
messages Father Brune studied in depth, and offers in this work, were
received by people without any connection to, or knowledge of, ITC.
Besides, at the time when the majority of such messages were received,
the new method of communication with the next dimension had not
yet been divulged by Frederich Jürgenson. The amazing French family saga starts before the end of the 1930s and continues until 1980 as
we saw previously.

A little further into the book, in a message from 1939, the communicating entity, this time Jean Winter (Gérald de Dampierre's uncle)
describes his plane of existence with these words: (literal translation)

My plane is not a little square board of 5000 or 1000 centimetres, it is
a space not closed, but which represents united souls with the same
degree of evolution. These souls are known or unknown; they are
lights that communicate with me as I communicate with them. They
are not little fellows who walk around. All and nothing happens, you
cannot compare the prisoner life of the body with the resurrection that
releases us from that body. Emptiness here [in our world], Resurrection
over there in the infinite beauty. I must say the same thing over and
over again. I sail, or I fly, or I float, as you wish.

And Jean Winter continues:

...that is: Head, Body outline, Glowing vapours. Each being is a light,
more or less intense, according to its evolution degree. Just imagine
glowing worms, large and very brilliant, among which you would
evolve incessantly, whose thoughts would be yours and yours theirs.
From it derives the exchange of ideas, of work. All this in the middle
of harmonious vibrations and you will have a faint idea of the stay of
the beings liberated from their bodies in the marvellous dwelling of
the liberated ... (Brune, ibid, 160-161).

This extraordinary description fits perfectly what my communicators have told me over and over again: "We are working; "We are all
here"; "We are very happy in our world"; "We are in heaven" and so on.
The voices rarely speak in the singular and if sometimes a voice, like
the one that identifies as my father's, or Só's, says "It is your father, João

Cardoso" or "it is Só", this is immediately followed by "It is us, it is all of us, it is the dead", etc. in the plural. I have also noticed that the communicating entities normally use the expression "here" when they are speaking with us and call their own world "over there" or use similar expressions. And again, this happens in media so distinctly different as ITC or mediumistic messages such as the French ones, as we just saw.

An Explanation

The message above speaks of "united souls" but in no way should this be understood as concerning human souls only. Our communicators' information is unanimously affirmative in this regard – from the French automatic writing messages to Adolf Homes' computer texts, to the Luxembourg contacts and my own – everything has a soul.

I believe we should forget the old, limited concept of 'soul', introduced by the different religions, and replace it as applying to energy and information. Something we cannot see but allows the physical to function. On the subject, the communicating Gérald de Dampierre on page 105 of Father Brune's book says:

> ... About death? What a real dire word indeed, so unsuitable *vis-à-vis* our life. It should be suppressed from the vocabulary forever. Firstly, it does not mean anything at all because even down here [on the earth] all is alive, even the rocks and grandfather Winter was very right about that....

Recapping, we find that the Group-Soul, the permission to contact us, the permission to discuss certain issues, the existence of hierarchies and strict rules in the next dimension, etc. have all been mentioned at least since the middle of the 19th century and are common to both reputable mediumship communications and ITC ones. In addition, the majority of the operators who received such messages, myself included, had no previous knowledge of the existence of the earlier mediumship reports, which say virtually the same. In my opinion the common, independent pattern thus revealed is a compelling argument in favour of the survival of consciousness to physical death hypothesis.

The Extraordinary Capacities of Next Dimension Beings

The nature of 'the other world' seems to account for a great number, maybe all, of the extraordinary possibilities and capacities that our dear communicators enjoy in their new life; for instance, being able to be in several places at the same time, to communicate by telepathy with all other beings – humans, people from other worlds, plants and animals alike – to travel with thought and so on. I once asked my communicators if those, for us, amazing capacities were the result of the death process or of their environment and they responded that they pertain to their world. This must be the reason why Timestream informed the Luxembourg group that a unique language was available to everybody immediately after the transition from our world. This is what the Technician had to say on the issue:

We all speak a language which is comparable to telepathy. When we speak to you we translate it into your Earth language. According to your human terms, our language consists of 27,000 characters. I am not considering the purely acoustical. Our language is immediately usable after bodily death.

Likewise, when I insisted with the communicators at the Bacci Centre in Grosseto, to speak with me in Portuguese instead of the Spanish they were using, I received the following explanation:

Because the world is big, take into consideration that there are so many languages; moreover, I am told that through the radio waves everything arrives; and by listening, I am told it changes into your language. (literal translation from the original DRV, mostly in Portuguese). (*ITC Journal* 25, April 2006).

The similarity is obvious. The unidentified entity that had been speaking with me in Spanish until then, finally spoke in Portuguese and gave me this fairly reasonable explanation about their difficulties with our earth languages. I found it particularly interesting that the masculine voice said: "… and by listening, I am told it changes into your language" because this seems to confirm the role of the operators' linguistic mental patterns in the process.

Rio do Tempo has informed that they are able to communicate with animals, plants and each other through telepathy. Since our dear transpartners avow that we hear their thoughts, I think we can put both explanations together and assume that under certain (unknown to us) circumstances, the radio waves act as a kind of transducer of their thoughts. And by listening, the earth operator – unconsciously tuning into the DRV communicators' 'frequencies'[9]1 – can understand the message in his or her language. These could explain why some operators, e.g. Friedrich Jürgenson, Dr Raudive and others who speak several languages (I among them) receive, or may well receive, information in several different languages.

In this theory, which I tentatively put forward, we are, however, left with the puzzle of finding out how the tuning may occur. It is possible that the synergy, between communicator/s and recipient, facilitates a kind of manifestation of the communicator's thoughts thus producing the radio voices. This could be a possibility but we cannot speculate further. Naturally, we are dealing, here, with concepts not yet tested in our world. But who knows if quantum physics will one day open this area of study to humanity? Let's hope it will happen soon, thus allowing the desirable and highly necessary paradigm shift to come about.

In my theory – I must emphasize that this is just a personal idea – the 'manifestation' of thoughts into radio voices happens mainly through love and deep interest acting as a kind of catalyst. But other reasons may concur. I am thinking of patience, affinities, self-sacrifice, persistence, endurance and so on, from both sides – the other dimension communicators and the ITC operators in this world. I have seen that some call it 'resonance'. Others speak of a 'field of contact'. Nonetheless, I still believe that the main thrust for these communications to happen is love and unlimited patience. And the latter is a direct consequence of the former. At Homes' the communicators recommended, "learn please to be patient: we can only do for you what you yourselves desire; and have sufficient energy for it ..."

At my home, a voice from Rio do Tempo station literally said "We speak por amor" (We speak through love).

In addition to the conditions that favour the contact field, or resonance, or tuning in – whatever we would like to call the meaningful connection between the communicators and the experimenter on the

---

9   The use of the word 'frequencies', as above, should be understood in the light of the explanations provided by the transcendental communicating entities at Homes', as we saw in a preceding chapter; they have no relation to our electro-magnetic frequencies.

earth – there is a requirement which appears to be important, also. I am thinking of the learning process that those who live in the next dimension must go through to be able to speak with us or, at least, to be able to speak well with us; this applies particularly to the DRV. I have recorded voices saying to each other, "You do know; so you must speak!" or "You speak! You know how to!" This might explain the following wonderful episode.

Nisha Speaks

My beloved female Doberman dog, Nisha, about whom I have spoken extensively elsewhere, has communicated with me on a number of occasions, always with a delicate, childlike human voice. On one of those instances, I addressed the communicators and commented "Rio do Tempo, how extraordinary that Nisha can speak so often!" (At the time she used to). A voice from Rio do Tempo replied to my remark with "Nisha learned to speak through the radio and she wants to speak with you!" A straightforward reply that our human prejudices prevent us from accepting at face value. As a matter of fact, the event, as much as it delighted and moved me, also surprised me as I am sure it will surprise many of my readers. And perhaps some will not believe it, although I absolutely guarantee that it is true (pieces of Nisha's contacts can be listened to in my CD 'Electronic Voices'). I was particularly astounded by the fact that Nisha always spoke via the DRV, which, as informed by our communicators, is a very complex method. But, as my communicators said, "she learned to speak through the radio", therefore, she could do it!

It was a truly amazing experience even for me, accustomed as I am to strange occurrences. Thinking about it now, years later, I reckon that my reaction was purely the result of what I blame on others – prejudice! And prejudice is something I am not generally prone to, as anybody who knows me, or even my readers, will recognize. But Nisha spoke with a human voice and it was a little too much for me. Since then, through the study and the continuing contact with the electronic voices and other sources of information, I understood that my Nisha's marvellous contacts must have been, above all, the result of love, determination and persistence from her side. Nisha was a very intelligent and curious dog. She must have had guidance, too, because during an earlier EVP contact, previous to the DRV, a feminine voice can be heard saying "Nisha, come on Nisha!" and finally a different, soft voice uttered, "Nisha!"

In his work that we have been following, Father Brune comments on a similar case – although this time a highly relevant message received from a dog by the medium Reynald Roussel:

> ... the second [explanation] is supported by Anne-Marguerite Vexiau's[10] works on 'psychophanie', as follows: The dog's emotions would have transited through the brain [mind] of a deceased or of Reynald's, and they would have transformed, through a kind of automatic process, into a very well-constructed sentence (Brune, ibid p. 196).

I must say that I partially agree with this explanation, albeit only to some extent because it contains the seeds of anthropocentrism, which I attempt not to allow in my mindset.

The clear content of the EVP by a voice which seemed to be teaching Nisha how to speak, appears to confirm Vexiau's suggestion but, in my opinion, only to a certain degree. I mean the voice that says "Va Nisha! (literal translation: Come on Nisha!)" is not necessarily related to a human; it can be a superior being encouraging and teaching Nisha to speak. We know that humans also need this training and help, which is generally provided by superior beings of a different nature, or by highly developed humans or beings of other species and origins. And we can find several pertinent examples in the history of ITC advanced contacts: the Technician in Luxembourg, the high nameless entities at Adolf Homes', Carlos de Almeida in my own case and Swejen Salter in Luxembourg, among others.

It is my deep conviction that we should set aside the prejudice of attributing all important feats to human intervention. As a high entity told Hans Otto-König, "You [Man] should realize that a plant or an animal can be a much more advanced spiritual being than a human."

The Problems Caused by Human Language

Later on, when I could deal with Nisha's contacts in a more liberated manner, I recognized that in order to speak with me, she could only

---

[10] See Vexiau, 1996, Je choisis ta main pour parler, Paris : Robert Laffont ; 2002, Un clavier pour tout dire, Paris : Desclée de Brouwer.

have used human speech since I do not understand any other. And, although I cannot fully explain to my readers how Nisha can speak human language – besides, she spoke in Portuguese and we usually spoke to her in English because she was born in India – the truth is that, as we have already discussed, ITC translates thoughts and emotions into language. Language becomes a mere tool, although indispensable, because we are unable to perceive our communicators' feelings and thoughts directly; but it is nothing decisive *per se.*

Furthermore, I think that we should consider the language corruption and mistakes, so often found in ITC communications, under this light. A good example is the corruption of the word "alma" (soul) during one of Carlos de Almeida's conversations with me. He clearly uttered in the middle of a longer talk: "Este mundo é o do "elme" que aposta noutro lado..." (Literal translation: This world is of the "soul" that bets elsewhere ...) See CD.

He said "elme" but must have wanted to say "alma", which is the correct word for soul. The word "elme" does not exist in Portuguese but phonetically it resembles "alma". The two vowels "a" have been replaced by the next vowel, "e". Since we do not know what process our communicators use for translating their feelings and thoughts into human language, and considering that the rest of the sentence appears to be related to the concept of soul because it is a "world that 'bets' elsewhere", – and 'bet elsewhere' is an expression which might be used in the sense of having different values – the language fault could very well be the result of the inadaptability of the communicators' feelings and thoughts to our language patterns.

While for us language and emotions, or ideas, are naturally linked, for our transpartners, emotions and ideas are predominant and they must search for the adequate word or words in a language mental pattern which no longer belongs to them because they no longer need or use it. Perhaps they search in the linguistic mental patterns of the operator's brain or in their own memories and this can cause added problems.

This might be a likely explanation, although the *modus faciendi* still remains open. And it remains open not only in regard to dogs but to humans or anybody who might speak through ITC, as well. Unfortunately, from our side, we have not much of value to offer on this issue. Let us hope that one day we may understand the process a little better.

Speaking of language, I should explain that I have used the term love in a non-personal way. Not love for somebody or something in particular, but all-embracing love; love for the next world, for life, for the communicators in general, for the well-being of all and the universe. Pure, universal love. Perhaps this is what Carlos de Almeida meant when he announced a few years ago, "It is to call upon love without gender; it is for humble people, it is to call upon love, panacea of the world, it would be beautiful, won't it?" (Translation from the original in Portuguese). I explained in my CD 'Electronic Voices' (DRV example 2) that the word 'gender' in Portuguese can be employed in a very wide sense. I also suggested that when Carlos de Almeida said "It is for humble people" he was referring to ITC's goal. But this is my personal interpretation. Other ones could certainly be applicable.

Chapter 11

WHAT ABOUT SUFFERING?

Every human being and perhaps other species, will worry about suffering sooner or later. Indeed, suffering seems to be insepara-ble from life on this planet. Not only bereavement, which might very well be the most devastating form of suffering, but other forms of distress can also have a heavy toll on us and, naturally, on other species of our wonderful planet. Amongst the most impacting causes of misery we find diseases, hunger, calamities, destruction of habitat, segregation, confinement, etc. all of them common to every being in this planet.

Unfortunately, we cannot properly assess the suffering of other species and, therefore, the majority of people ignore their plight. This leads us not only to concentrate our views and our complaints on hu-man suffering, but also to consider that only human pain and sorrow exist. A great mistake because the suffering of other species can be as painful, and I believe, in many cases even more painful. Such a nar-row view of life is a shame on humans because it means, basically, that we cannot fully absorb the majesty of life, besides feeding our lack of sensitivity and compassion which is, of course, highly damaging to our growth as a species.

When, years ago, I started receiving DRV contacts and could speak with Rio do Tempo fluently, one of my main concerns was to find out about suffering. I have seen so much suffering – human but principal-ly non-human – that I desperately attempted to find out if there was something beyond it. I was tormented by the reasons, if any, for it. Was it all random? Was it devoid of any meaning? Why did it happen? It seemed to be a law of Nature and nothing in Nature is useless but I tried in vain to understand the reasons. What about the innocent beings, all the beloved little animals I had seen going through unbearable pain and anguish? Their stunned, pure eyes asking why kept turning round in my head causing me great anxiety.

Also, some of my beloved family members had gone through the ordeal of cruel illnesses or the trial of apparently unjust, dreadful circumstances that destroyed their lives. It all made me question bitterly the cruelty of life for I could not make sense of it.

Thus, whenever I could, I would ask Rio do Tempo why such terrible misery happened to innocent beings. Above all, I viewed it as something extremely unjust and injustice is one of the situations that disturb me most.

Rio do Tempo did not answer my query for some time. Then suddenly, one evening, when again I asked if suffering had any meaning, a serious voice replied "It has all, it has all the meaning." And on yet another occasion, a grave voice replied to my question as to whether suffering was important for spiritual growth with "It is very important!"

At the Harsch-Fischbachs', the high entity whom we call the Technician stated:

> The pain that humans must experience and bear represents a part of their own self. It is due to one's personal actions or it is wanted by a superior power. In both cases it serves to kick off the study process leading to knowledge, to betterment and to perfection. (Harsch and Locher, *Les contacts vers l'Au-delà à l'aide de moyens techniques existent!* French edition, 1995, pp. 143-144).

Also via ITC, this time a message from Axel, the deceased ten-year old grandson of the French ITC pioneer Monique Simonet, confirmed, "I did not suffer in vain, Mummy. Suffering helps not only personal evolution but also others, because we are all connected." And on another occasion, "Remember, I said that suffering is never useless: it favours evolution ..." (Simonet, 1991).

Also in France, one of the automatic writing messages that we have been looking at, received on June 21, 1939, said:

How much trouble in human lives and how wonderful deliverance is; but there is deliverance and deliverance; it is preferable for some to continue living in order to expiate through suffering and thus earn the magnificent stay. (Brune, ibid p. 163).

In the beautiful book *La Troisième Oreille: À l'écoute de l'au-delà* by the world-famous clairvoyant, Marcel Belline, he tells a story about the telepathic communications with his only son, Michel, who died tragically at the age of twenty. Here, we find a similar explanation. The boy's mother was terribly distraught after the tragic happening, and Belline persistently tried to contact the boy but he succeeded only after twenty months. To Belline's question, "Michel, can you help us live?" The boy replied "No, but you must live ... My death has only meaning through your suffering and your survival." (p. 110).

What else could be more explicit about the bonds that tie us all and the role of suffering in life?

For a long time – perhaps because I associated it with stories of karma and other esoteric tales, which I do not particularly like – I resisted the idea that life is to be understood as essentially transcendental; although in my deep inner self I felt this was the way. At the bottom of my contradictory attitude was the fact that from one side, the materiality of the life we know is obvious. And from the other, the majority of us are educated to strive for the things that matter in our society: money, social position, good health, good looks; overall, the quality of life and happiness we hope for is based on possessions, comfort, power over all other beings and natural forces – mountains, rivers, oceans, forests and so on. All that exists on the earth must submit to human ambition and greed. Understanding, knowledge, perception, sensitivity, communion with Nature and all the other beings, open-mindedness to the unknown are never considered. However, our dear communicators tell us that, essentially, these are the things that matter.

Thus, suffering is rejected in our present-day society. It is considered the ultimate, meaningless aberration. I am not a religious person, certainly not a Christian and, therefore, I believe that I cannot be accused of transplanting Christian ideas about suffering, starting with redemption and the martyrdom of Jesus Christ at the cross, to the information I receive from my ITC communicators. But the truth is that our transpartners tell us, by many different ways, to many different recipients, that suffering is an invaluable tool to open the doors of consciousness. And even if our modern world tries by all means to contradict this idea, claiming that suffering must be avoided at any cost, that we were born to be happy, that death is the ultimate tragedy etc., I am deeply inclined to believe my communicators.

Chapter 12

FINAL REMARKS
REINCARNATION, DEATH,
GOD, LIFE

Some of ITC transmitted information corroborates Eastern and Western mystic traditions – reincarnation among them. Other information goes beyond the teachings I am acquainted with. However, I must confess that I am no expert on ancient traditions; thus, maybe some Vedic texts have a similar approach.

Reincarnation

ITC messages do not speak of systematic reincarnation but rather of selective rebirths. The major, most comprehensive ITC communications have thrown some light on this controversial subject. In Luxembourg the Technician assured the experimenters.

Even if you dislike the idea, it is as I tell you: reincarnation exists. Reincarnation means progression and not regression. Animals, also, are subjected to the cycle of reincarnation.

At Rivenich, the messages received by Adolf Homes teach us:

An unlimited multiplicity of experiences and possibilities is open to the souls. Reincarnation is one of many. Through reincarnation the individual has again the possibility to fundamentally better his own soul. Thanks to reincarnation processes, the possibility of conducting the conscience to positive paths is continuously offered to the individual ...

And about the soul:

The spirit of the primigenial God creates souls and worlds in psychical and physical forms and structures. Each being in the universe is endowed – in its totality – with soul. The essence of the soul as well as the Omnipotence of God exceeds any possibility of expression. The soul has a multidimensional way of living. It is formed of many billions of extremely minute psychic particles which are found in the multidimensional field. The soul is absolutely not the consciousness. Indeed, your brain has nothing to do with your soul. Instead it is your consciousness which is linked with your brain. In its turn it is the soul which is more [connected] with your consciousness. Your consciousness is therefore only a small part of your soul ...

The subject of reincarnation used to upset me. I have always found the idea rather unpleasant. Initially I used to dismiss it as some oriental nonsense. And, naturally, when the ITC contacts happened, I could not resist questioning Rio do Tempo about it. Their straightforward reply to my – "Does reincarnation exist?" was – "Only when there is no other way". And I thought this implied that reincarnation only takes place when there is no other way of progressing. It kind of relieved me because I must confess that I am not a big enthusiast of life in this world the way we have developed it. Although I have been blessed in many ways, I find it very difficult to cope with the sufferings most of us go through, with injustice, cynicism and the violence we witness on a daily basis against those who cannot defend themselves – animals, nature and feeble humans. So, reincarnation does not appeal to me but this was the reply I got; and it agrees with other ITC messages such as the ones I quoted above.

Similarly, a good friend of mine, also an ITC experimenter, a medical doctor of good intellectual capacities and culture, albeit, unlike me, very attached to Spiritism, asked, during her EVP session, if re-incarnation existed. To her great surprise, a masculine voice replied clearly, "From time to time". She was surprised because for her, based on the Spiritist teachings she had adhered to, reincarnation was the law, not a sporadic event.

Naturally, reincarnation is directly linked with death because to re-incarnate, at least in this world, it is necessary to die.

Death

My ITC communicators avow that the hour of death is predeter-mined. An unidentified voice from Rio do Tempo confirmed, in reply to my question about the time of death, "Anabela o tempo está mar-cado, podes dar o passo e o compromisso ... está marcado para toda a gente ... " (Anabela, the time is predetermined, you may take the step and the commitment, it is determined for everybody ...). I did a literal translation and the oddness of the language is obvious because "take the step and the commitment" is not a sentence we normally use in this context.

When my first book, *Electronic Voices* was published, I received a letter from a well-known parapsychologist who had tried to replicate EVP voices, with negative results. In his letter he mentioned that the information conveyed by the voice I cited above contradicted the in-formation he had received from a medium whom he much admired. It said that we 'choose our time of death'. I presume that, unsurprisingly, his use of "we" applied to humans only. In any case, I am not preoc-cupied with what mediums of whatever rank say. I transmit factually what my communicators tell me and I am happy to let my readers de-cide what to do with the relevant information.

In the French compilation of the automatic writing messages that we have been looking at throughout this book, Jean Winter imparted this:

> I have said that [in a previous message], to avoid the thoughts of those who could feel – if the Beyond is such happiness, life is not interesting. Those people would, then, live only materially without fighting, without joys, without the obligation of struggling in order to deserve death. But to live is necessary; to fight is necessary; the time of death is not chosen by us, it is unnecessary to dwell on this [topic] ... (Brune, ibid p. 250).

The text made me smile because the expression "the obligation of struggling in order to deserve death" is used in exactly the opposite way of what we normally do. We say, for instance: what did he or she do to deserve death? Meaning what crime, what wrongdoing did he or she do. But the other world communicator, Jean Winter, used it in the sense of having to work, to endure, to deserve the wonderful gift of death. What a different perspective. On November 20, 1940, Jean Winter conveyed the following:

> Everything is predetermined, free will exists for little things; you have the liberty of gaining or losing your future happiness, but the hour of your death and the main facts of your existence, you cannot prevent them.
>
> (BRUNE, IBID, *LES MORTS NOUS AIMENT*, P. 273).

As expected, we find also many comments about death in the Homes' messages. I will translate a short excerpt of those.

> All spirit includes all life, since there is nothing dead. There is no dead matter. There is only the physical death of the flesh. Simply the process of transformation of the psyche takes place. The death of the body does not derive from justice or from injustice but from the interaction in the interior of God's omnipotence. After the death of your body the psychic consciousness of the soul passes into the pluri-dimensional information, which is not subjected to any form of separation or death ... (Senkowski, German original p. 85, Italian translation, p. 79. 1999).

And the communicator from Rio do Tempo station who spoke with me about "the other pure world" (see chapter 6) finished that evening's contact with the following information: "We have no death. We have only one death!"

God

This is a subject of the greatest interest for a large majority of people and, therefore, I will convey some extracts of the information received by different ITC operators, allegedly from superior beings.

I have already touched on the subject of God throughout the book, including the few comments I received from Rio do Tempo on the issue.

Further to these, information of great significance was communicated to Adolf Homes, purportedly by higher beings with great knowledge and wisdom. They addressed the subject from two different angles. From one side there is what they call the "Divinity", or the "God of the Origins", the principle, which is the source and totality of all that exists. The source, the principle, cannot be described or understood, either by us or by the other world communicators even the higher beings in question. God is all that is and is beyond any possibility of expression. There is nothing else to say.

Then, also according to Homes' communicating entities, there are the "pseudo gods" or "secondary gods", the gods of all religions, created by man to serve his own purposes, and very much as a result of the human fear of death. Those anthropomorphic gods have manipulated to disturb the divine order of the origins, the Truth, as the communicators also call the "God of the Origins".

The essence of the Homes' messages is comparable with the Technician's explanation in Luxembourg, namely, "Man forms God according to human images and conceptions. God or the principle cannot be compared to anything." (Locher and Harsch, 1989)

Strolling through the enchanting Père Lachaise cemetery in Paris, some months ago, I saw the tomb of a famous personality (most of the tombs there are of very famous people) and although I cannot recall who it was – only that it was a famous French scholar – I remember very well the inscription on the mausoleum wall, which read, "God is your consciousness".

The phrase impressed me, since, as one of the best descriptions of God I have seen. But very recently, I found another impressive, and somehow complementary interpretation of the concept of God. The explanation, allegedly received by Dr McKay from his deceased son Jordan, said:

> I knew, for example, that the purpose of life was learning. But I had no idea that the wisdom each individual soul acquires contributes to the wisdom/knowledge of collective consciousness (the divine/god). I had no idea that each lesson in our lives allows – ultimately – collective consciousness (god) to make the next, more perfect universe. (Tymn, 2016).

I was stunned because practically identical thoughts had been lingering in my mind for quite some time, well before I read this text.

As an agnostic I have trouble in accepting the transcendence revealed through our ITC contacts. During the long hours mulling over all that happened and its meaning, I imagined that an experiential, evolutionary god – a creative, dynamic force that would psychically absorb and transform the good and the bad experienced by all beings in this planet (and certainly in many others) and feed on those cosmic experiences, constantly to evolve – would make some sense to my critical lay mind. Thus, I was thrilled to see a similar interpretation conveyed from the next world. Naturally, nothing tells us this is the truth; once again, it may be only one probability in an infinite scenario of multiple possibilities.

Life

Anybody attempting to pierce the veil of mystery that surrounds the magnificent gift of life that we humans, and our companions on this planet have been endowed with has, most likely, reflected on the meaning of life. In spite of the difficulties and hardships involved, I say 'the gift of life' because our dear communicators have emphasized that the most important tool for progression and development is "time and space"; in our case therefore, life here on the earth.

Hence, it is a privilege to finish my work of compilation and comparison of messages coming, apparently, from the next level of existence and received, mostly, through ITC, with extracts of the information received at Adolf Homes' computer on the topic of life.

Further to the immense informational value of the latter, my citations of Adolf Homes' materials are also intended as a heartfelt tribute to my very dear friend Professor Dr Ernst Senkowski, a key figure in the research, study and disclosure of Instrumental Transcommunication. He granted me free access to, and free use of, these and all other materials he assembled, studied and published during his long and rich life among us. Here is an extract of the Homes' messages about life:

Life is love. Love is life forever. Every life is sacred and much beyond a human representation. All that lives, and everything lives, is part of creation. The thoughts live, the dead live, the computers live, everything lives. Every life is fulfilled thanks to transformation. Every life in the worlds, even the most diverse, searches for unlimited perfection. All forms of consciousness live eternally, therefore also all beings that you call animals. Every life (including animals, plants, minerals, genders of gross matter and subtle matter) consists solely and absolutely of information. The information of the unconscious is the living message of the universe. In the worlds live innumerable beings. Because nothing disappears, in you and among you live all the gods and all the saints. You will reach the understanding that your dead live among you. The dead live in a parallel way.

All that is interesting for life in your planet comes at the utmost in all dimensions. The harmony of all that lives here, in positive as well as in negative, creates all forms, known and unknown.

Life and death in your concept of time are a tiny bit in the infinity of the Spirit. Life is equal to situation. Your present life on the earth can be considered a kind of flash visit. There is much more life than we all believe. But it is all similar to your life. Everything is formed of atoms. Atoms, which continuously disappear and are born, bring new life in every form. Organic chemistry is omnipresent. We exist in the ocean of all living consciousnesses and we are who we are. You live in the space of an illusion that we call time. Everything consists of incessant experimentation. We can also say that every life in your planet is a continuous experiment made by other intelligences. And remember that as it is true that you are, so it is true that we are, and many others who in turn live in other realities. For us, who are alive like you, your life means probability in an omnipotent reality without the concept of time. Allow, I beg you, love to decide your life because without love your life is like a bell that does not ring. Please do not lose the courage even if your life seems disheartened. Love and patience can assume live forms. The sun that allowed life to be will burn it; then, can the earth destroy the sun? The physical end is not far away because the man of the earth has lost his dignity and forgotten his task, since you are living in a world which, in great measure, you have contributed to create. In the long term life on the earth is no longer possible. The father is not responsible for all the life of his sons."

(SENKOWSKI, GERMAN ORIGINAL, PP. 49-50. 1999).

I believe that accepting the logic of paradox with expanded consciousness is the key to crossing the threshold of the path of understanding. The adventure of discovery and exploration of the magnificent electronic voices starts here. "Why do you look for the living among the dead?" This biblical sentence appeared many times in Adolf Homes' messages and I believe it is a good way of closing this book because, indeed, there is only life.

References

Bander, P. (1972). *Carry on Talking.* Gerrards Cross, UK: Colin Smythe.

Bander, P. (1973). *Voices from the Tapes.* New York: Drake Publishers Inc.

Barrett, Florence (1937) *Personality Survives Death.* London: Longmans, Green and Co.

Belline, M. (1972) *La Troisième Oreille: À l'écoute de l'au-delà*, Robert Laffont, p. 110.

Bender, H. (1970). Zur Analyse aussergewöhnlicher Stimmphänomene auf Tonband. Erkundungsexperimente über dir « Einspielungen » von Friedrich Jürgenson. *ZSPP (Zeitschrift für Parapsychologie und Grenzgebiete der Psychologie)*, 12, 226-238, Freiburg i. Br: Walter-Verlag.

Bender, H. (1976). *Verborgene Wirklichkeit.* Munich: Deutscher Taschenbuch Verlag.

Bose, J. (1902). Response in the Living and Non-Living. New York: Longmans Green.

Bose, J. (1913). Researches on Irritability of Plants. New York: Longmans Green.

Bose, J. (1926). The Nervous Mechanism of Plants. New York: Longmans Green.

Brune, F. (1993). *Les Morts nous Parlent.* Paris: Ed. du Félin, Philippe Lebaud (1st ed. 1988).

Brune, F. (2005, 2006). *Les Morts nous Parlent*. (3rd. Ed.) Tome 1 (2005), Tome 2 (2006). Paris: Oxus Editions.

Brune, F. and Chauvin, R. (2003). *À L'Écoute de L'Au-Delà*. 2nd. Ed. Paris: Oxus.

Brune, F. (2009). *Les Morts nous Aiment*. Agnières: Éditions Le Temps Présent.

Cardoso, A. (2003). Survival research. *Journal of Conscientiology*. Vol. 6, n° 21, pp. 33-63.

Cardoso, A. (2005). Translation of the transcript from the two original recordings made by Marcello Bacci and Anabela Cardoso at Grosseto on 5 December 2004. *ITC Journal* 21, pp. 25-33.

Cardoso, A. (2005). ITC: personal results and guidance on methodology. In Cardoso, A. and Fontana, D. (Eds.). *Proceedings of the First International Conference on Current Research into Survival of Physical Death with Special Reference to Instrumental Transcommunication*. Vigo, Spain: ITC Journal Publications.

Cardoso, A. (2006). Marcello Bacci interviewed by Anabela Cardoso. *ITC Journal*, 25, pp. 19-22.

Cardoso, A. (2007). Instrumental Transcommunication – Contact with another reality potentially open to all. *Proceedings of the Second International Conference on Current Research into Survival of Physical Death with Special Reference to Instrumental Transcommunication*. York, England: Saturday Night Press Publications for ITC Journal Research Center, Vigo, Spain.

Cardoso, A. (2007). The Overwhelming Spread of Instrumental Transcommunication Contacts of High Quality. *ITC Journal*.

Cardoso, A. (2010). *Electronic Voices, Contact with Another Dimension?* Ropley, Hants, UK: John Hunt/O-Books.

Cardoso, A. (2012). A Two-Year Investigation of the Allegedly Anomalous Electronic Voices or EVP. *NeuroQuantology* September 2012 Volume 10, Issue 3, pp. 492 -514.

Cardoso, A. and Fontana, D. (eds.) (2005). *Proceedings of the First International Conference on Current Research into Survival of Physical Death with Special Reference to Instrumental Transcommunication (ITC)*. Vigo, Spain: ITC Journal Publications.

Carrington, H. (1907). *The Physical Phenomena of Spiritualism*. Boston: Small, Maynard & Co.

Cummins, G. (1932, 2012). *The Road to Immortality*. London: Ivor Nicholson & Watson; 2012 ed. USA: White Crow Books.

D'Argonnel, O. (1925). *Vozes do Além pelo Telefone*. Rio de Janeiro: Pap. Typ. Marques, Araújo & C.

Estep, S. (1988). *Voices of Eternity*. New York: Fawcett Gold Medal Book, Ballantine Books.

Estep, S. (2005). *Roads to Eternity*, Galde Press, Inc. PO Box 460, Lakeville MN 55044, USA.

Fernández, C. (2006). *Voces del Más Allá. ¿Hablan los Fallecidos a través de los Equipos Electrónicos?* Madrid: Editorial Edaf S. A. (El Archivo del Misterio de Iker Jiménez).

Fontana, D. and Cardoso, A. (2002). Developing a protocol for DVR. *ITC Journal*, 12, pages 55-57.

Fontana, D. (2003). Le ricerche sull T.C.S., con particolare riferimento al l'opera di Anabela Cardoso. *La Richerca Psichica* X, 3, 232

Fontana, D. (2005). *Is There an Afterlife?* Ropley, Hants, UK: John Hunt/O Books.

Fontana, D. (2009). *Life Beyond Death*. London: Watkins Publishing.

Fuller, J. G. (1985). *The Ghost of 29 Megacycles*. London: Souvenir Press Ltd.

Gettings, F. (1986). *Encyclopaedia of the Occult*. London: Rider & Co.

Grandsire, J. M. (1998). *La Transcommunication*. Agnières: JMG éditions.

Gullà, D. (2005). Computer-Based Analysis of Supposed Paranormal Voices: The Question of Anomalies Detected and Speaker Identification. In A. Cardoso and D. Fontana (eds.) *Proceedings of the First International Conference on Current Research into Survival of Physical Death with Special Reference to*

Instrumental Transcommunication (ITC). Vigo, Spain: ITC Journal Publications.

Gullà, D. (2007). Voice signal enhancement: processing and postprocessing.

In A. Cardoso and D. Fontana (eds.) *Proceedings of the Second International Conference on Current Research into Survival of Physical Death with Special Reference to Instrumental Transcommunication (ITC)*. Vigo, Spain: ITC Journal Publications.

Holbe, R. (1987). *Bilder aus dem Reich der Toten*. Munich: Droemersche Verlogsanstalt Th. Knaur Nachf.

Jacobson, N. O. (1973). *Life without Death?* New York: Delacorte/Seymour Lawrence.

Jürgenson, F. (1964). *Röstema från Rymden* (Voices from the Space). Stockholm: Saxon & Lindströms.

Jürgenson, F. (1967). *Sprechfunk mit Verstorbenen* (Freiburg im Br.: Verlag Hermann Bauer. Republished 1981 by Goldmann Verlag (München).

Jürgenson, F. (1968). *Radio och Mikrofonkontakt med de döda*. (Radio and microphone contacts with the dead) Uppsala: Nybloms.

Jürgenson, F. (2004). *Voice Transmissions with the Deceased*. Stockholm: Firework Edition N° 101. The Jürgenson Foundation: http://www.fargfabriken.se/fjf/

Kardec, Allan (1857). *Le Livre des Esprits*. Paris: Dentu.

Kardec, A. (1864). *Revue Spirite*.

König, H. (2007). Psychic structures as connections to other realities. In A. Cardoso and D. Fontana (eds.) *Proceedings of the Second International Conference on Current Research into Survival of Physical Death with Special Reference to Instrumental Transcommunication (ITC)*. York, England: Saturday Night Press Publications on behalf of ITC Journal Research Center, Vigo, Spain.

Laszlo, E. (2008). *Quantum Shift in the Global Brain*. Vermont, USA: Inner Traditions.

Laszlo, E. (2008). An Unexplored Domain of Nonlocality: Toward a Scientific Explanation of Instrumental Transcommunication. *Explore*, September/October, Vol. 4, N° 5, 321-327.

Laszlo, E. with Peake, A. (2014). *The Immortal Mind: Science and the Continuity of Consciousness beyond the Brain.* Rochester, Vermont, USA: Inner Traditions.

Locher, T. and Harsch, M. (1989). *Les Contacts vers l'Au-delà à l'aide de moyens techniques existent!* Association Suisse de Parapsychologie et Cercle d'Etudes sur la Transcommunication du Luxembourg (original German ed. 1989; French ed. 1995, Agnières: Parasciences).

Locher, T. and Harsch, M. (1992). Transcomunicação. São Paulo: Editora Pensamento.

Mancuso, S. and Viola, A. (2015) *Brilliant Green: The Surprising History and Science of Plant Intelligence.* Washington, DC: Island Press.

Puhle A. (2014) *Light Changes.* UK: White Crow Books.

Raudive, K. (1968). *Unhörbares Wird Hörbar – Auf den Spuren Einer Geisterwelt.* Remagen: Reichl.

Raudive, K. (1971). *Breakthrough: An Amazing Experiment in Electronic Communication with the Dead.* Gerrards Cross, England: Colin Smythe.

Schäfer, H. (1989). *Brücke Zwischen Diesseits und Jenseits.* Freiburg: Verlag Hermann Bauer KG.

Schäfer, H. (1993). *Ponte entre o Aqui e o Além - Teoria e Prática da Transcomunicação.* São Paulo, Editora Pensamento (Portuguese translation of the above mentioned work).

Scott Rogo, D. and Bayless, R. (1979). *Phone Calls from the Dead.* Englewood Cliffs, New Jersey: Prentice-Hall.

Senkowski, E. (1995). *Instrumentelle Transkommunikation* (first Ed. 1989) Frankfurt: R. G. Fischer.

Senkowski, E. (1999). Die Transkontakte des Adolf Homes – Ein rückblick. Teil 1: übersicht und transpartner (The transcontacts of Adolf Homes - A review. Part 1: Synopsis and Transpartners). *TransKommunikation.* Vol. IV, No.1, pp. 12-31.

Senkowski, E. (1999). *Transcomunicazione.* Available from Dr Carla Castagnini, Strada Statale Romana Nord, n° 135, I -41010 Fossoli di Carpi (MO), Italia.

Simonet, M. (1991). *Images et messages de l'au-delà*, Éditions du Rocher, p. 80.

Stead, W. (1922). *The Blue Island.* Internet Archive BookReader.

Swedenborg, E. (1853). *Compendium of the Theological and Spiritual Writings of Emanuel Swedenborg.* Boston: Crosby and Nichols, pp. 160-197.

Théry, P. (2000). First telephone contact in France by Konstantin Raudive. *ITC Journal*, 2, 42-43.

Tymn, M. (2013). Difficulties in Spirit Communication Explained by Dr James Hyslop, *ITC Journal*, 47, 63-84.

Winter, J. and Dampierre, G. (1939). Messages inédits. *Le Messager*, 61, 7-8.

Wright, S. H. (1998). Experiences of Spontaneous Psychokinesis after Bereavement, *JSPR*, 62, 385-395.

Wright, S. H. (2002). *When Spirits Come Calling* (Ch. 9 Lights that blink a message). USA: Blue Dolphin Pub.

Zimmer, H. (1962). *Myths and Symbols of Indian Art and Civilization.* New York: Harper & Row. pp. 24-26.

INTRODUCTION TO THE
APPENDIX

The present study constitutes a landmark in ITC research. My
affirmation may appear as a lack of modesty but it is nothing of
the sort. Although I was the person in charge of devising and
organizing the study, the whole project is a collective enterprise, not
an individual feat.

We received the invaluable trust and financial support of two important international organizations and counted on the collaboration
of several ITC operators who came from different places in Europe
to take part in this study. Furthermore, the School of Engineering of
Vigo University, in Galicia, Spain kindly allowed us to use their excellent acoustic facilities and their sound equipment. My gratitude goes
to all of them.

Readers are invited to follow the development of the research in the
report published by *NeuroQuantology*, which I hereby reproduce with
the kind permission of its Editor.

All details of our work are carefully described, step by step, without
omitting, or masquerading, any event.

The conclusions speak for themselves. It is possible to obtain and
record anomalous electronic voices under tightly controlled conditions
and using neutral facilities and devices that did not belong to any of
the ITC operators involved.

Furthermore, the voices recorded were all pertinent to the operator,
to the environment or to the project context. It is true that the voices

were louder and more frequent when the conditions of the experiments were relaxed and uncontrolled. But, and this is the most important conclusion: they were also obtained when the conditions and the recording environment were the strictest possible.

The current investigation shows, beyond doubt, that the electronic voices are real, much further than the anecdotal level which has, unjustly, been labelled on them by many parapsychologists and by the public in general. The majority of the people belonging to both groups do not have the knowledge, the preparation or the feedback that would allow them to make proper statements about the subject. This is a matter of utmost importance for humanity and for the world in general and it should not be dismissed easily without proper information.

I take great pleasure in offering my readers the possibility of deciding by themselves about this amazing phenomenon, which clearly points to the reality of the survival of consciousness to physical death.

I warmly thank the NQ Editors for allowing the publication of the report in this book.

A Two-Year Investigation of the Allegedly Anomalous Electronic Voices or EVP

by Anabela Cardoso

Republished from NeuroQuantology | September 2012 | Volume 10 | Issue 3 | Page 492-514

ABSTRACT

A relatively novel acoustic phenomenon has inundated the Internet and specialized literature. Several Associations, some of them with an important number of members, have formed around it in many countries. In the Anglo-Saxon world the phenomenon is called EVP (Electronic Voice Phenomenon) and is usually assumed as electronically mediated communication from or with the deceased. The first tests aimed at verifying the reality of these claims were carried out in Sweden and in Germany, in 1964 and 1970, under the direction of Professor Hans Bender from Freiburg University (Bender, 1970; 1972; 2011).

The present report describes in detail the tests designed to record the allegedly anomalous electronic voices, or EVP, under controlled acoustic conditions. Series of experiments were carried out in Vigo, Spain throughout a period of two years under conditions controlled to the highest degree achievable. Several operators were involved in the many tests conducted in Acoustic Laboratories and professional recording studios equipped with very high levels of acoustic shielding. The protocols and procedures followed in the experiments, as well as the results obtained, are herewith described. Several extra voices were recorded during the many experiments performed for which no normal explanation was found.

Key Words: DRV, EVP, acoustic background support, anomalous electronic voices, carrier, frequency mixture, noise, phoneme mixture, transcommunication

Corresponding author: Anabela Cardoso

Address and about the author(s): The author wishes to express grateful thanks to the operators who generously and enthusiastically participated in the present research project and, very particularly, to Professor Uwe Hartmann for his technical assistance. Also to Stanley Krippner, Ph.D., and Alan Watts Professor of Psychology, Saybrook University, San Francisco, California, U.S.A. for his invaluable support. The research was made possible through the financial contribution of two international sponsors who wish to remain anonymous. Their generous support is gratefully acknowledged. Mail to: anabela@itcjournal.org. Received May 19, 2012. Revised June 21, 2012. Accepted Sept 9, 2012. eISSN 1303-5150

Introduction

Controlled experiments aimed at the recording of the purportedly anomalous electronic voices (EVP) were carried out in Vigo, Spain, during the years 2008 and 2009. Dr. Anabela Cardoso (2010) was the research project director and also the main operator of the EVP tests.

The tests were inspired by Hans Bender's work with the Swedish artist and film director Friedrich Jürgenson (1964; 2004) and by Dr. Konstantin Raudive's experiments in England, documented by Colin Smythe's Associate Editor, Peter Bander (Bander, 1972). In 1968 Raudive published *Unhörbares Wird Hörbar – Auf den Spuren Einer Geisterwelt* and a few years later the English translation *Breakthrough: an Amazing Experiment in Electronic Communication with the Dead* (Raudive, 1971) followed.

Before bringing out this translation, the English publisher, Colin Smythe, arranged for Raudive's work to be put to the scientific test.

With the technical assistance of electro-acoustic experts Ken Attwood and Ray Prickett and in the presence, among others, of Colin Smythe, Peter Bander, Sir Robert Mayer, David Stanley, Ronald Maxwell, Raudive himself, four tape recorders (the principal recorder being made by Nagra, a Swiss company, and said to be well shielded from radio interference) were set to record for 18 minutes under the supervision of the aforementioned experts from Pye Records. In his book Bander describes the experiments and affirms that "instruments revealed recordings were taking place although the listeners [*monitoring the recording in real time through their headphones*] could hear nothing.

On rewinding and playing back the tapes, over 200 voices, of which 27 were clearly understandable, were heard".

A second series of experiments was held in the screened chamber at the laboratories of Belling and Lee, in Enfield, England. This laboratory was equipped with a shield for radio frequencies designed to prevent the intrusion of electro-magnetic waves. Peter Hale, the top British expert in electronic frequencies screening techniques and one of the best in the world, together with Ralph Lovelock, physicist and electronics expert, supervised the recordings during which a series of clear EVP voices was again captured. In his letter to Colin Smythe, Peter Hale said about the tests: *"From the results we obtained last Friday, something is happening which I cannot explain in normal physical terms."*

(Bander ibid, 1972). A large number of Raudive's recordings have been preserved in Münster, Westfalia, in Germany, and another collection has recently come into the possession of the British Society for Psychical Research and subsequently given by them to the British National Acoustics Laboratory.

Both Jürgenson and Raudive claimed to record the voices of the deceased who, according to Raudive, live in an alternative level of reality that he called "the opposed world". EVP voices sound like human voices and cannot be heard directly while the operator is doing his/her recording experiments. They are audible only on playback.

EVP experimentation usually consists of one or more operators who do their recordings, on a regular basis, in a quiet site without extraneous noises. During the recording session they request a contact and ask questions from communicators of an unknown dimension of life where the deceased are also supposed to go on living. The session takes normally 15 to 30 minutes, with each question being followed by a short period of silence and then another question is asked.

There are also reports, albeit rarer, of anomalous electronic voices coming directly from the loudspeaker of a radio (Cardoso, 2010). They are called Direct Radio Voices (DRV) but these are not specifically in the scope of the current research project.

Since the time of Jürgenson's and Raudive's experiments, there has been an increasing number of reports, from all over the world, of people who claim to receive the voices of the deceased through electronic means. While a good number of those reports might be attributed to pareidolia, there are others which deserve attention and should be examined carefully, since the reported communications seem to carry the meaning attributed to them by the operator and other listeners

(Brune, 2005; 2006; Brune and Chauvin, 1999; Cardoso, ibid 2010; Cardoso, CD, 2010; Locher and Harsch, 1989; Senkowski, 1989; 1995).

Method

The Operators

A diversified pool of operators from different parts of Europe was selected. Names and abbreviations of the operators follow: from Portugal: Anabela Cardoso (AC), Luísa Alcântara, Maria dos Anjos Antunes, from Germany: Ingrid (IH) and Uwe Hartmann (UH), from Spain: José Ignacio Carmona (Iñaki).

They were all experienced EVP operators with positive results who had never experimented together. This seemed a good way to test the possibility of recording the allegedly anomalous voices under what are considered, in the specialized literature, unfavourable conditions. It seems that an important requisite for these communications is the so-called 'contact field' which, apparently, is based upon a special synergy between operator/s, equipment, location and communicators. In this study all the sites chosen for the tests were unknown to the operators. Most of the equipment used belonged to the recording facilities of the selected institutions and, therefore, was unknown to all the operators. A couple of pieces of apparatus were the private property of Anabela Cardoso (AC) and did not fit into this description but those will be duly identified.

Series of recording sessions were scheduled, taking into account the operators' availability to come to Vigo, Spain. Besides AC nobody in the group lived in Vigo (some had never been in the town before) and, therefore, the tests were scheduled for different dates throughout the two-year period.

The operators were not alone in the recording room. Philip Newell (PN) or another Sound Technician, or both, were present throughout the experiments, either in the recording room or in the adjacent technical room (see diagram of the Metropolis facilities below).

Location of the Tests

The tests took place in two different professional acoustic studios and were supervised by more than one sound technician. The premises were chosen because of their very high level of sound isolation, in order to guarantee the maximum possible acoustic shielding of the environment where the experiments were going to take place. They are among the most sophisticated in the region of Galicia, Spain, where AC currently lives.

The University of Vigo was the first choice since the School of Telecommunication Engineering has a Laboratory of Acoustics with top levels of sound isolation and also a hemi-anechoic chamber (www.teleco.uvigo.es). Associate Professor Antonio Pena (*Theory of the Signal*), in personal correspondence to Anabela Cardoso about the levels of acoustic shielding of the Laboratory, informed her:

"...The background noise in the interior of the chamber shows us that the acoustic shielding is very high. Its construction suggests it - a block of concrete suspended over dampening materials and isolated from the rest of the surrounding building."

Philip Newell (PN) was technically responsible for the construction of the University Acoustic Chamber. Consulted by AC about the acoustic shielding of the Lab, PN informed:

...I know that there is at least 70 dB of isolation from the adjacent rooms. Music at 100dB in the control room is inaudible in the [acoustic] chamber, next door". And, in one of his technical reports, he informed: "...It was also noticeable that nobody's mobile telephones had any coverage in the heavily acoustically isolated laboratory ...

Nevertheless, given the nature of the project designed to test purportedly anomalous phenomena, still regarded with prejudice by the mainstream scientific establishment in Europe, the pre-condition for the use of the University facilities was the assurance that there would be no direct involvement of its academic institutions or researchers in the work. The University facilities were put at AC's disposal for a limited period during summer holidays, when there were no students or classes. Thus, the main recording room of the professional Vigo Sound Studio Metropolis was also hired for the tests.

The Metropolis was designed, like others in the UK, Spain, Portugal and other countries, by Philip Newell, international expert in sound isolation. PN's expertise is interference-free recordings (http://philipnewell.net). In one of his technical reports, said PN about the Metropolis:

It has also been reported in much of the [EVP] literature that domestic recorders function just as well, and perhaps better, than professional recording systems. This could be due to higher levels of crosstalk and lower levels of screening allowing more possibilities for the reception of signals, which the equipment was not intended to pick up. However, in the studio where our current experiments are taking place I, personally, designed the audio cabling installation, the electrical power installation and the acoustics. It was all done in a way that was designed precisely to reject external interference, in order to achieve the cleanest possible recordings. The question began to arise as to the degree to which this heavily screened system could even reject the capture of signals of a nature which had not been envisaged in the design of the studio (EVP and DRV).

... As prior literature had reported transcommunication [EVP] experiments even being made with radios tuned to the medium wave band, around 1 MHz, then it could probably not be said that all of the earlier tests made in the so-called Faraday cages had been definitively shielded from external radio pick up. In the studio in which we were experimenting in Vigo [the Metropolis], however, just about every part of the recording chain was shielded from *any* normally unwanted radio-frequency pick up.

The Technicians

As aforementioned, Philip Newell is a British electro acoustics engineer and shielding expert who lives in Galicia. Further technical assistance was provided by Metropolis sound technicians and by the Portuguese sound designer Marco Lima (ML). Prior to the experiments, all the technicians were unknown to AC and to the other operators.

Equipment

The main equipment used in the tests belonged to the institutions where the tests were performed. An old analogue Telefunken mains powered cassette recorder found by AC in an antiques shop was also used in some experiments, connected to a Sennheiser microphone. The following equipment was used at the Metropolis in 2008: Neumann U 87 condenser microphone in its omnidirectional mode, Shure SM 58 moving coil microphone, Digidesign ProTools recording system in a Mac computer, a Telefunken mains powered cassette recorder (property of AC), a Sennheiser miniature omnidirectional microphone and power supply (property of AC), Three diode circuits constructed by PN.

In 2009 at the Metropolis, the above, with the exception of the diode circuits plus a Sennheiser MD441 microphone with preamplifier brought by experimenter UH from Germany, were used.

The following equipment was used at the University of Vigo in 2008:

The system of the Acoustics Laboratory: a Brüel & Kjael 4190-L001 (Falcon Range $1/2^2$ Microphones — Types 4188 to 4193) measuring microphone and pre-amplifier, connected to a Fostex R-DAT recorder. According to PN, "the system was 3 decibels down at 1.5 Hz, and hence could capture four of the infrasonic octaves."

The Sennheiser microphone connected to the Telefunken cassette recorder as above described.

The following equipment was used at the University in 2009:

Microphones

Sennheiser MD 441 hyper cardioid (used with a preamplifier). Brought by experimenter UH from Germany.

AKG C414 XLII in cardioid's pattern (property of ML).

Groove Tubes GT57 in figure eight pattern (property of ML) connected to ML's laptop computer, via a mixer (Xenyx802, 8-input, 2- bus Mic Preamp), through the heavily mounted wall between the acoustic chamber and the technical room.

AC's laptop used to produce explicit noise inside the acoustic chamber.

For the measurements of the electrical and magnetic fields:

3D H/E Fieldmeter ESM-100 by Maschek, Germany, frequency area of the measurement: 5Hz-400kHz, 2 values per second (property of UH's University) connected to UH's laptop in an adjacent room.

Noise Sources

Experience indicates that noise is possibly a carrier, or at least a beneficial factor, for the formation of the anomalous electronic voices. A lot has been written about it in the specialized literature.

Each recording situation is normally composed of implicit noise (background noise: noise of the environment, acoustic and electronic noise of devices, noise produced by the EVP operators, such as breathing or stomach noises, etc.) and explicit noise added by the experimenters. In order to reduce environmental noise to the largest extent, the present experiments were carried out in heavily acoustically shielded rooms. In addition, in order to differentiate between the noise of the devices, the noise unconsciously produced by the operators and the explicit noise played by the experimenters, separate observations were carried out.

Several kinds of explicit noise can be applied in EVP experiments. In the present experiments the following were employed as acoustic background, one at a time:

a) Frequency mixture:

Random frequency-mixture can be created by computer programs, the so-called pseudo noise.

1. Audio files with two types of noise - white noise and pink noise - were included in the present experiments.
2. Random static noise, also called 'white noise', obtained from a radio tuned between stations was also used in some experiments.

b) Phoneme mixture:

1. Some EVP operators, also called experimenters, use a mixture of fragments of words as explicit noise during their recordings. Audio files of this kind can be generated by a computer program called 'EVP-maker'. This program, developed by Stefan Bion, became lately very popular for EVP experiments. The functional principle is based on a simple idea: an audio recording of human speech is cut into short segments, which are rendered randomly. If the initial audio recording is made of natural speech, the result sounds like "random speech" i.e., a random mixture of phonemes or of syllables. Some parameters, like the length of the segments, can be adjusted by the program. The aim and apparent advantage of this technique versus the well-known 'white noise' method is to get a human speech-like background for EVP recordings without any real words or sentences, i.e., without any semantics[11]. And the hope is to present an acoustic energetic stimulation for

---

[11] The use of this method will be discussed later in the report

the formation of EVP utterances, within, above, or together with the random speech sounds.

2. The Psychophone. The apparatus was an invention of Austrian scientist Franz Seidl for the reception of the alleged transcendental voices during his experiments with Raudive (Breakthrough pp. 362-365). See circuit diagram below.

3. Human speech, either in the form of live conversations or of a computer file recorded with human voices.

DIAGRAM OF PSYCHOPHONE

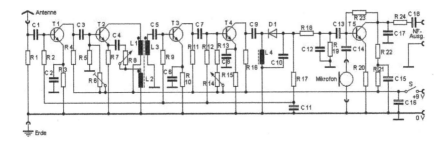

The Tests

In 2008, several experiments were carried out.

1. With AC as the sole operator

In June 2008 four experimental recording sessions aimed at EVP reception took place at the Metropolis, between 20.30H and 21.30H.

These were held on June 12, 17, 24 and 27. The experiments were invariably performed with the doors of the recording studio closed. The facilities were used in exactly the same way as for professional recordings.

Three diode circuits were constructed by PN in metal boxes according to the diagrams in Professor Alex Schneider's Appendix to 'Breakthrough' (see pp. 341). The circuits were built with components close to those described because the precise diodes used in the 1960s are no longer generally available. The diodes were used in some of the June recordings connected to the analogue tape recorder.

The first experiment took place on June 12. It consisted of a casual conversation between AC and PN in the role of participant in the experiment. The moon was waxing. Conversations, with or without questions to the presumed communicators, were one of the methods used by Konstantin Raudive in his experiments in England (Bander ibid, 1972) and by Friedrich Jürgenson in the experiments designed and controlled by Professor Hans Bender during which some extra voices were found commenting on topics of the conversation (Bender, 1970; 2011). Both the condenser and the dynamic microphones were connected to the studio's digital recording system. The computer room is also acoustically isolated; it is separated from the recording studio by a double-glass window and double insulated heavy doors. The analogue system was directly operated by PN in the studio where the experiment took place. PN connected a microphone to one of the tracks of the cassette recorder and one of the diodes to the other track of the machine. Both pieces of apparatus were simultaneously recording on the same blank tape, each one on a different channel, left and right. No additional noise was added to the environment. No extra voices were detected in the first test realised.

On the 17th of June, once again at sunset, another recording session was carried out at the Metropolis studio. The weather was hot and clear, and the moon would be full the next day. The first experiment of the day – on average each recording test took between 15 and 20 minutes, and two or three recordings were normally done in each session – consisted of a casual conversation between AC and PN without any explicit background noise.

In the next recording AC experimented alone in the studio while the sound technician Iago supervised the recording in the computer room. This time AC decided to follow a different protocol. The random noise produced by a Sony ICF-SW7600GR radio tuned between stations and by a transformed 'broad band' radio receiver, which cannot be tuned to radio stations and yields a hiss (Cardoso, 2001) were used as acoustic background for the experiments. The Sony radio was tuned to 7,249 KHz because this frequency seemed to cause less mains interference (PN had found out that the radio charger was defective and this produced much electrical interference).

At the beginning of the test AC stated that the project was an updated replication of Konstantin Raudive's work and asked: "... *can Dr Konstantin Raudive hear me?*" During her brief talk, the radio started to produce voices and AC mentioned the fact loudly for the information to be registered on the recordings, thinking that a radio emission had managed to get through. As soon as AC finished her initial remarks about Konstantin Raudive, the radio voices surged, AC again mentioned the fact and lowered the volume to its lowest, actually thinking that it was a radio emission.

The sound technician in the adjacent computer room had also heard the voices while recording. The masculine voices were low and disturbed by electrical interference, apparently caused by the charger; they could not directly be understood.

When the experiment finished, AC and the sound technician listened to the recording and understood that the voices spoke in Portuguese. The loudest words sounded like: *"Está no estúdio"* followed by, almost imperceptible, *"aqui"* (File 'U_87_03' at 00: 01': 37"). Translation: "[He] is in the studio (here)". These words were followed by a singing cadence that seemed to say *"falamos p'ra...?"* (We speak for...). The first very soft, blurred words audible, could be interpreted with uncertainty because the amplitude is low and the signal to noise ratio very poor as: *"o Konstantin Raudive ..."* (Konstantin Raudive ...)". The amplitude of the voices is approximately -31, 5 dB[12]. Since AC's question had been if Konstantin Raudive could hear her, this seemed to be a reply. Could it have been an anomalous Direct Radio Voice (DRV)? To assess this possibility, the important point was to be sure of the content of the radio voices and this was the next step in the investigation.

The audio file was submitted to several listening tests by Portuguese nationals and by professional listeners, as was the case of Rafael, the chief sound mixer at Sodinor (a dubbing film studio in Vigo), and other sound specialists. The listening tests took place at the Metropolis' well isolated listening facilities, and the content was confirmed. The people involved in the listening tests are regarded as experienced listeners. None of them was familiar with the DRV. The most trained ones spontaneously understood the words *"Está no estúdio"*. On the whole, the audio clip was heard and scrutinized by several dozen people. Their conclusion acknowledged that the signal to noise ratio was quite poor and confirmed the words: *"... está no estúdio"* and *"falamos"*. We can ponder that if AC had directly understood the content of the radio voices, she would not have lowered the volume of the radio as she did.

---

[12] All amplitude values mentioned refer to the peak values measured by Sound Forge Pro 10.0 software.

We can also hypothesize that the radio voices replied to AC's question about Konstantin Raudive and, in that case, would be anomalous.

No voices were heard or detected in the next experiment in which PN also participated. The radio hissing noise, now tuned to 7,248 KHz, was used as acoustic background.

On June 24th, at 20:00, one more set of experiments was carried out at the Metropolis. The moon was waning and the weather was partially cloudy. This time only the condenser microphone was connected to the digital recording system. The two analogue tracks of the cassette recorder were set for the diodes, which were recorded digitally from the line outputs of the cassette recorder. Some whispers with apparent semantic content were identified but, in spite of the fact that the majority of the voices recorded in the presence of Professor Hans Bender with Friedrich Jürgenson as main operator "were revealed by the analysis of the sounds with Visible-Speech-Diagrams to be at the threshold of human auditory capacity" (Bander ibid, 1972), very low whispers will not be taken into consideration in the scope of this research project. No proper voices were detected in this test.

On June 27 another set of tests was done at the Metropolis. The diodes were connected to the Telefunken cassette recorder and this time both the condenser and the dynamic microphones were connected to the digital recording equipment. The waning crescent had been on the 26th.

On this occasion a most beautiful voice that could not be heard coming through the Sony radio used as a source of background random noise - now tuned to 7,429 KHz and producing a soft hiss - appeared recorded on the computer hard disc. It was heard by the listening team only during playback. It was a soft feminine voice with great reverberation that seemed to speak from the bottom of a long, wide tunnel and sounded like uttering in Portuguese the following sentence: "*Somos nós (Luís)*" (Translation: "It is us (Luís)". This time AC experimented together with PN, and all her questions and comments were in English.

The voice was captured by both the dynamic and the condenser microphones and although, as usual, the recording levels were set at the same value for both microphones, the Shure SM 58 recording is much lower (the utterance has peak amplitude of - 41.6 dB). As happened throughout the experiments, although lower, the sound seems to be more defined in the dynamic micro file than in the condenser file with a peak of -19.5 dB (Files SM 58_05 and U 87_03, minute 07':20"). This is most likely due to the characteristics of the microphones. The voice appeared in the recordings after AC finished one of her questions with "... is this correct,

Rio do Tempo?" AC understood the first two words of the three word sentence "*Somos nós (*possibly: *Luís)"* the first time she heard it. The last word is not clear because much softer and it sounds like progressively diluting from a strange spatial positioning. Further auditory tests by a group of Portuguese nationals, the chief sound mixer of Sodinor above mentioned and two sound technicians of the Metropolis confirmed the understanding of the words "*Somos nós*" but no unanimous agreement was reached about the third word (probably '*Luís*' but '*Sim*' for some) in result of its very feeble amplitude. Interestingly Luís was the name of AC's deceased brother and the 27th of June was the date of his birthday.

In the test that immediately followed, the second of the evening, AC mentioned Luís' birthday and asked if her brother could reply to her. It should be emphasized that no listening had yet been performed when the second test took place and, therefore, the sentence "*Somos nós (Luís)"* had not yet been detected. The coincidence between the date and the word "Luís" can be interpreted as:

- pro: the word "Luis" is indeed related to the date.
- con: when trying to identify a meaning, subconscious thinking may lead to that word.

This second test was done with the noise produced by both silicon diodes amplified through the electronics of the cassette machine, passed through a mixing console and fed back into a loudspeaker, so that the sound of the diodes was passed into the air and mixed with AC and PN's voices digitally recorded by the two microphones. PN described the "new system" in the recording proper (Files 'U 87_04' and 'SM 58_06'). No extra voices were found.

About the two voices recorded in June, said PN in his Technical Report N° 2:

"... From all the tests made and analysed in June, only two voices remained unaccounted for. The first was captured via a Neumann U 87 microphone, digitally recorded by a Digidesign ProTools system. Despite the fact that there was no unanimous agreement about what the voice was saying, none of the staff of the recording studio could recall ever having captured such a voice during any normal recording [of the studio], and no attempt to re-create a similar sounding voice was even vaguely successful. The second voice, of a soft but highly reverberant nature, was captured simultaneously on June 27th via the Neumann U 87 condenser microphone, and a Shure SM 58 moving coil microphone. Recordings made simultaneously on the cassette recorder, via two different diode circuits (Nos. 1 and

2), showed no sign of the voice. No explanation could be found for how a softly spoken voice could penetrate the acoustic isolation of the studio, and *within* the studio there were no reverberant spaces. A test was arranged for July to listen for external voices from the studio's surroundings, to see if any similar sounding voices could be detected ..."

And in his Technical Report N° 3 PN summarizes:

> ... In short, nothing whatsoever was captured which in any way resembled the two anomalous voices in question, and we could think of no ways to recreate anything similar to them. Furthermore, the female voice with reverberation (the second of the two voices under discussion here), captured on June 27th, had a sound character which it was difficult to imagine to have come in any normal manner through the small loudspeaker of the short-wave radio that was being used as a background noise source at the time. The voice had an open sound which was totally uncharacteristic of the radio (a Sony ICF-SW7600GR), and, what is more, nobody in the room at the time of the recording, (Añabela and myself), who were less than two metres from the radio, recall hearing anything of the voice at that time.

The November Recordings

On November 13 around 17:00H another experiment with AC as the sole operator took place at the Metropolis. The weather was bright, cool and the moon was full that same day. Sound technicians PN and Marco Lima (ML) were also present.

The big innovation this time was the use of the psychophone. PN built the machine according to the diagram in *Breakthrough*. A microphone was directly connected to the psychophone, the output of which went directly into the ProTools digital recording system. The psychophone did not emit any sound into the air. The other systems – the usual Metropolis condenser and dynamic microphones, as well as a dynamic cardioids microphone brought by ML and set up in a MS system (recording SE 4400 8 Figure) were also set up to record independently but simultaneously with the psychophone. No analogue recordings were made.

Besides the voice of the operator captured through the microphone input, the psychophone captured also a mixture of radio emissions, which could be heard during the playback of the recording. None were heard live from the air. Several seemingly anomalous voices were recorded which were detected upon playback. Some of those even seemed to have a characteristic Portuguese accent and to say pertinent things such as "Ela é portuguesa?" (Is she Portuguese?), or, translation: "You came from another world", etc. However, they will not be considered for the purposes of this research project because, being so mixed up with the radio voices proper, pareidolia could occur and it would be too risky to vouch for their paranormality.

Conspicuous noises, apparently not produced in the controlled recording environment, appeared recorded this time. The sound of scratching, which could have been produced by AC's pencil writing on paper to show the time to PN, is immediately followed by the sound of tapping, and a series of three raps similar to a table tennis ball jumping on a hard surface precedes very fast voice whispers. During the first months of her experimentation in 1998, AC recorded very similar knocking sounds that apparently were not produced in the recording environment (Cardoso ibid 2010).

There is also a voice whisper which seems to be constructed with noise and was easily detected in the microphones and in the psychophone recordings. It is inserted inbetween the abovementioned noises and it seems to reply to AC's question in English: "Is the psychophone a good way for your EVP messages?" The whispered sentence sounds like: *"Contacto pode fazer no rádio"* (Contact you can make in [through] the radio). (Files PSICHOPHONE Line_02 at 05':00", SM 57 Dynamic_02, U 87 Condenser_02 and SE 4400 8 Figure _02 all at minute 04':59"). The psychophone inclusion sounds more modulated, more like a proper voice while those registered by the other microphones, of the same content, sound more like vocalized noises. In the MS recording system the whispers are practically imperceptible. When the apparently anomalous whispered voice finishes, a loud knock can be heard in the recordings. At the end of this particular session, PN stated loudly for the record that, during the works, he was absolutely concentrated on environmental noises and none could be heard, while ML added that he had done the same and only a couple of stomach and saliva noises had been produced by AC, PN and himself.

2. Experiments with AC and the Portuguese Operators Luísa Alcântara and Maria dos Anjos Antunes

The first recordings took place at the Metropolis. The experimental recordings proper used white noise artificially produced as acoustic support and yielded no significant results. However, totally clear and loud voices that did not belong to the people present appeared recorded when the small group of people that included the two Portuguese operators, this author, Philip Newell and Francisco, Luísa's husband, were preparing another experiment that would use human voices as background noise.

Since Dr Konstantin Raudive and Friedrich Jürgenson used controlled conversations in their recordings (Bander, 1972; Bender, 1970; 2011), an experiment using voice phonemes was devised. It is assumed that the sound of human voices facilitates the production of the anomalous electronic voices. This assumption is based upon the premise that the communicators use human phonemes as the 'raw material' from which they produce their utterances, and it seems to be at the origin of the EVP-maker software. Although, as aforementioned, the method is currently favoured by many EVP operators, the use of human phonemes in whatever form increases the probability of pareidolia. This factor should be taken into careful consideration when analysing the results.

Preparation for the EVP Experiment with Human Phonemes as Acoustic Background

The experiment proper was designed to use human phonemes of informal conversations between operators and participants, recorded live in the acoustically shielded recording studio of the Metropolis. For this purpose the group invented sentences and engaged in illogical, funny conversation; some recited poems. AC decided to have the conversation file thus obtained reversed and use it as acoustic background for the experiment proper that would follow. The idea behind the reversing of the recorded conversations was to provide a background of human phonemes, without semantic content, for the formal experiment and thus test the latest fashion among EVP operators as above said.

This preparatory, informal recording took place at the usual hour of the tests, around 21.00H, on July 26, 2008 in the main recording studio of the Metropolis. The moon was in the waning crescent the day before. As usual, all the doors were closed in the studio. The five people present – AC, Luísa Alcântara, Maria dos Anjos, Francisco (Luísa Alcântara's husband) and PN – deliberately chatted nonsensically as explained.

Very unexpectedly, sentences uttered by voices that sound very different from the operators' and participants' were found in these informal recordings. One of those, of exceptional clarity and intelligibility, seems to be of a young boy and says: *"e um pouco envergonhado"* (Translation: and a little ashamed [timid]). It is preceded by a feminine voice that clearly says *"já estou a ficar nervosa"* (I am already getting nervous); the clear feminine voice in Portuguese is apparently very different from the voices of the three women present. It appeared recorded in the middle of a sentence in English spoken by AC. AC's speech seems to have been abruptly cut out and replaced by the aforesaid sentence in Portuguese, in a kind of overlapping of AC's voice. However, at the end of what would have been AC's talk, the two voices can be perceived simultaneously – a fragment of AC's voice and the last phonemes of the extra feminine voice. The juvenile, boyish voice that says *"e um pouco envergonhado"* comes next and is followed by still another voice that whispers something not easily decoded because it is muffled. In some way these sentences resemble a conversation going on between two or three people, not physically visible, that observe and comment on what is happening in the studio because ten or so seconds later, AC pressured PN saying "Philip say things!" Until then, PN had been rather quiet, not participating in the nonsensical talk going on. To this PN replied timidly: "... it is difficult under strange circumstances".

These startling acoustic occurrences started at minute 02':29" of the files recorded by different means – the condenser and the dynamic microphones and the analogue tape deck (Files Audio 2_01, condenser_02, dynamic_02, of July 26, 2008) – and continued for almost five seconds.

In the course of the same informal recording, another very interesting voice that does not sound similar to the operators' or to the participants' voices and, similarly, comments directly on what is happening in the room appeared recorded at minute 03:07". AC had just scolded Francisco for being quiet and pushed him to speak, laughing and saying loudly in Portuguese: "so the men are all quiet, what is happening here?" At this point a masculine voice appeared recorded that says clearly and loudly in English: *"This is hot!"* It is distinctly understandable, while Maria dos Anjos softly recites a poem in Portuguese in the background. It was registered by all the apparatuses[13]. The conversation between operators and participants above described was animatedly carried out in an atmosphere of laughter and excitement.

---

[13] Although neither very closed microphones nor a laryngograph for each participant were used, it is possible that forensic tests can determine if the voices under analysis here belong to any of the participants in the conversation.

Without being previously listened to, because they were not part of any proper test but only intended for use at the next formal EVP experiment as acoustic support, the files were digitally reversed by the Metropolis sound technician and played as background noise in the proper EVP experiment with questions that followed.

The extra voices in the original babble files were detected in subsequent listening purely by chance, in view of the fact that the recording was not part of the formal tests, and, therefore, not meant to be submitted to listening scrutiny but just reversed for subsequent use.

The reversed files used in the EVP experiment proper were later compared with the original non-reversed babble files which, fortunately, had been saved to the computer hard disk of the Metropolis.

Formal EVP experiment using reversed human voices as acoustic background

A puzzling occurrence happened in the formal experiment that used the reversed voices as acoustic background. At minute 03':40" (Files 'Condenser_03' and 'Dynamic 3 _03') operator Maria dos Anjos asked if somebody was listening to her and could he/she give a name. Fifty seconds later and immediately before she asked her next question, Francisco's reversed voice can be heard saying clearly *"Felipe"* (Philip); this is followed by a two seconds pause and his voice continues *"Felipe da Silva"* (Philip da Silva), a name and surname in Portuguese. The original audio file was checked and it showed that exactly at this point Francisco stuttered, mispronounced a word and repeated it. Since Francisco does not normally stutter, this episode appears even more interesting because the stuttering and repetition of a specific word allowed for the formation of a name and surname in time to match the operator's question and request, i.e. before her next question. It would be of great interest to consider the "odds to chance" involved in this chain of acoustic events and obtain a p-value.

Experiments with the Same Operators at Vigo University Laboratory of Acoustics

The tests took place on July 28, 2008 between 13:30H and 15:00H. The moon was still waning. In his technical report, said PN about the

University experiments: "One set of recordings was made with a CD recording of white noise as the background, reproduced via the full audio-frequency range loudspeakers of the laboratory. Later recordings were made using the aforementioned Sony radio, tuned to 13.600 kHz as the background source. The aerial was folded. It was also noticeable that nobody's mobile telephones had any coverage in the heavily acoustically isolated laboratory, which, being alongside the radio frequency laboratory, shared much of its shielding. Nothing but a smooth random noise was heard emanating from the radio. After the recordings, the DAT was copied to CD, which was transferred the next day to the ProTools system in Metropolis studios. The audio cassette was also fed into the ProTools system the following day."

As usual, the experiments consisted of a series of three or four questions put by each operator to supposed communicators. Each question was followed by a period of silence of between one and two minutes, and then another question was asked.

In the experiments with white noise, a couple of alterations of the white noise were detected. Those were easily perceived as whispers with linguistic content by the listening team constituted by AC, ML and Rafael, the Sodinor chief sound mixer abovementioned. The amplitude is very low (around -32,5dB while the white noise recorded by the DAT is in the region of -34dB). The clearest of the utterances was recorded during AC's experiment and it seems to be a pertinent reply to the question asked by the operator in English at 04':57": "... are you also here today, with us, in this studio of the University of Vigo?" The masculine voice whispers in Portuguese, at 5': 07,9" of the digital audio file (File 'Extract from CD 2 - Track 3 ANABELA') and 16': 24,3" of the analogue recording: "Está aqui o Cardoso" ("Cardoso is here"). "Cardoso" is the surname of AC's deceased father, brother and other paternal family. AC's deceased brother, a Merchant Marine captain, was usually called "o Cardoso" by his colleagues instead of his full name, Luis Cardoso, which they never used. The utterance is audible both in the DAT University recording and in the Telefunken tape recording (Files 'Tape Audio 1_01.L.' and 'Tape Audio 1_01.R'). The sound is cleaner in the digital recording perhaps because it is free from machine and tape noises but it is louder in the cassette recording, being understandable at direct listening without amplification (-25,4dB while the background white noise immediately preceding it was registered at -27,2dB). Subsequently to noise cleaning with Sound Forge Pro 10, the content became clearer and is easily understandable by anybody who knows Portuguese sufficiently well.

No whispers or voices were detected in the formal tests that followed using the Sony radio hiss as acoustic background.

However, apparently anomalous, clear voices were recorded when the first formal EVP experiment with Luísa Alcântara finished. Philip Newell disconnected the analogue machine but not the digital equipment, exchanged a couple of words with Luísa and opened the studio door. Next, a screeching metallic sound can be heard in the recording, immediately followed by a clear, well-structured feminine voice that says in Portuguese: *"Estamos aqui por cima"* (literal translation: "We are here above") at -33 db. This is followed by what sounds like the shouted voice of a youngster that seems to resonate from far away and says *"Só isso!"* at - 36 db. ("Only that! [That's all]"). Before this last voice, almost at the sub-acoustic level, a kind of faint pre-echo with the same content can be perceived with proper amplification (File 'Extract from CD 1 - Track 2 LUISA ANJOS' at 06':49").

The tests were done during the Summer holiday season and besides PN, the three operators and Francisco, there was nobody else in the big building of the School of Engineering where the Acoustic chamber is located. Considering the unmistakable semantic content of the sentences in Portuguese, which can clearly be understood by any native of the language, their peculiar sonority and the fact that they bear no similarity to the operators' or the two men's voices, it seems that these voices can be considered anomalous acoustic events.

3. Experiments with the Spanish EVP Operator Iñaki

From the 5th to the 8th of August 2008 the well-known operator José Ignacio Carmona (Iñaki) came from Toledo to participate in the research work (Carmona, 2010). This operator experiments without any additional background noise and monitors the whole recording live with headphones.

Tests at the Metropolis on August 5

On August 5 there was a new moon and around 19.30H Iñaki experimented alone at the Metropolis without any explicit background noise. AC and PN stayed in the recording studio with him but did not speak. The environmental noise of the room recorded by the condenser microphone during the experiment was around -50 to -52dB, and - 56 dB and less by the dynamic microphone. The voice of the operator often displayed -35 dB of amplitude in the dynamic microphone recording.

Perhaps the most interesting incident of this afternoon was the recording of what sounds like footsteps. Everybody sat quietly in their chairs, without moving, throughout the experiment. Although Iñaki did not mention it while he recorded, as soon as the test finished he told AC and PN that he had clearly heard the sound of footsteps through his headphones at some point of the recording (nobody else heard it). It was indeed found that rhythmic beats had been digitally recorded at minutes 03':15" by the condenser and dynamic microphones. The Telefunken cassette deck registered the same noises at minute 02':50". The analogue recording is quite louder (around -24 dB) and the sounds can be perceived at direct hearing without amplification. The sound of the three beats immediately precedes what seems to be the noise made by the springs of the operator's chair. Although the studio has top class acoustic isolation, it is extremely difficult to decide on the possible anomalous nature of the beats.

Iñaki at the University Lab on August 6

As had happened the day before, Iñaki chose to record without any explicit background noise. The recordings were again carried out with the professional technical equipment of the University and with the Telefunken machine connected to the Sennheiser microphone handled by Philip Newell. AC was also present. The tests started at 14.15H. Several remarkable incidents were registered during this experiment. From minute 12'42" to 12'47" the experimenter requested the invisible communicators to reproduce the sound of footsteps recorded the day before at Metropolis. At minute 12':56, 9" (2 Pista de Audio.L) the sound of what could be taken to be two footsteps can be heard, although at lower amplitude than the day before, followed by the sound of a bang a few seconds later (13':18,6").

The sound of the 'footsteps' cannot be perceived directly in the analogue recording, although the sound of a bang can also be heard in the analogue recording although lower ('Audio1_01.L').

At minute 15'45" the experimenter asks if the communicators wish to give testimony of their presence in any way. At 15':53,6" there is one low knock which is immediately followed by five clear and fast knocks (easily and directly audible in both recordings).

At minute 17':57" of the same file the operator asks if the invisible communicators are able to read his thought, and at minute 18':04" what sounds like a soft masculine voice whispering in Portuguese "*Somos capazes sim*" ("We are able, yes") can be heard. The amplitude is very low, -44dB only; it needs to be increased significantly and noise cleaned for some intelligibility.

At minute 22': 48" the sound of what clearly resembles three dog barks was recorded by the University DAT, while only one bark is apparent in the analogue recording. This is perhaps the most interesting acoustic occurrence of the afternoon because, six seconds later, the operator addresses his deceased dog 'Golfa'[14] and begs her for a sign, a bark, some evidence that she is near. The 'barks' have an amplitude of -37, 5 dB and can be heard directly. After being slightly amplified the sounds were presented, without previous suggestion, to several inexperienced, normal listeners. They were identified immediately by more than a dozen people as 'dog barks'. Since there was no dog inside or around the chamber (or even in the deserted building) and, besides, dog barks cannot penetrate the heavily mounted acoustic shielding of the Laboratory of Acoustics, it seems legitimate to conclude that these sounds can be classified as anomalous. Furthermore, the incident could speculatively, but meaningfully, be associated with the inclusion above-mentioned that affirms the communicators are able to read the operator's thought and with the operator's request to his dog for a sign of its presence.

The whispers with presumed semantic content detected often appeared before or after involuntary physiological noises produced by the operator such as the saliva, breathing or empty stomach ones or by a slight rotation of the chair. One of the chairs made a clinking sound when the operator moved on it. These minor noises can easily be checked in the recordings. None of them can account or be mistaken for the 'dog barks' above-mentioned.

The next informal experiment was performed with PN recording the murmur of Iñaki's and AC's conversation while they walked in the long corridor of the building. The Acoustics Laboratory double doors stayed open, so that the mumble of the operators' voices could reach inside the chamber and allow PN to record it – File '3 Pista de Audio.L'. There was nobody else in the big building of the School of Engineering

---

[14] All questions put by the operators to the purported communicators were not prepared beforehand but spontaneously asked during the experiment.

where the Acoustics Laboratory is located. Philip Newell went for a walk to check on this and, when he returned, announced loudly so that it could be recorded by the machines: "There is nobody else in this place".

As had happened with the Portuguese experimenters, apparently anomalous voices were recorded during this informal experiment. They started at 0'16" of the audio file mentioned with a clear sentence by a masculine voice that says in a mixture of the local Galician and Spanish "Ment[r]es[15] paseo yo en Vigo!" ("In the meanwhile I'll wander through Vigo!"), immediately Iñaki remarked that his personal DAT machine had been left in the recording mode saying: "... and my recorder continues recording, well that's all right, I'll check it later".

A few seconds later, at 00':26" of the digital recording, while AC and Iñaki were still speaking in the antechamber of the laboratory before heading to the corridor (PN remained inside supervising the machines), a very different masculine voice whispers in Portuguese: "Há passagem" (There is passage). Was this 'passage' a reference to the fact that the voices could get through? It could be interpreted as such.

Twenty-three seconds later, at 00':49,7", immediately following AC's comment in Spanish "Ya está!", and while the resonance of the last phoneme of AC's loud voice can still be perceived in the recording, two very beautiful feminine voices speaking in Spanish, one of which says: "Per[o][16] huye" ("But [he] runs away") and the other, very melodious, with great reverberation: "No cree!" ("[He] does not believe!") appeared recorded in both systems. AC had come back to check that the door of the chamber remained open and said "Ya está" (It's done) after holding the door with a piece of wood. The operators thought that the content of this 'conversation' of unknown origin could be regarded as a reference to PN who is not well disposed toward the voice phenomenon.

What could be interpreted as "O Luís é surpresa" ([For] Luís it is surprise) uttered by a feminine voice is registered at minute 2': 03", seeming to overlap Iñaki's and AC's voices chatting. AC's deceased brother's name was Luís, as aforementioned. At minute 02': 25, 6" of the same file, a singing masculine voice appeared recorded which seems to say in Portuguese "Lá vem Luís!" ("There comes Luís!"). The two operators, AC and Iñaki, return to the Acoustics Laboratory some twenty seconds later. The voices mentioned ("O Luís é surpresa" and "Lá vem Luís!") will not be considered for the purposes of the present research

---

[15] The 'r' is practically inaudible.

[16] The 'o' of the word "pero" is not audible.

project because they are too muddled with the operators' voices and it would be too risky to vouch for their paranormality. However, they appear to be anomalous and are mentioned with the aim of throwing some light into the voice phenomenon, which seems to benefit from a somehow chaotic, uncontrolled physical environment. They are much clearer in the University digital recording than in the cassette recording.

In the next formal experiment AC and Iñaki experimented together at the Acoustics chamber. It was digitally recorded at '4' and '5 Pista de Audio L'. A couple of apparently anomalous whispers were detected in this recording. The most obvious of those was in reply to Iñaki's remark addressed to Jürgenson, Raudive, Germán de Argumosa and other famous EVP pioneers. He finished with: "now, from the other side, you [they] can testify that the contact is feasible". The question finished at minute 07': 41" and, at minute 08':04" of '5 Pista de Audio L.' a very feeble utterance that seems to say *Era o contacto...*" ("It was the contact...") appeared recorded at -43 dB of amplitude. The natural sound of the environment during the experiment oscillated between -44 and -45, 6 dB. As said before, the Spanish operator records without any additional noise source.

Throughout the experiments, the whispered utterances recorded without any additional acoustic background are lower than the ones recorded with an acoustic support. The former must be similar to "the low amplitude, taped-recorded voice effect" described by Bayless, for which he emphasized the need of "high amplification" (Bayless 1980, Scott Rogo and Bayless 1979).

At the end of the experimentation PN properly drew the operators' attention to the metallic noise one of the chairs could make and that was deliberately recorded for comparison with unidentified metallic noises that might appear in the recordings.

Iñaki Goes to the Metropolis Again on August 7

The experimentation started at 14.20H with both operators very tired from the intensive work of the preceding days. The moon would be in waxing crescent the next day.

In one of the experiments, an audio tape copied from a professional music CD that mixes dolphins' shrieks of joy with sounds of water and soft melody was used as background acoustic support. The tape was copied to the computer hard disk before the experiment in order to be compared with the recordings that used it as background noise. AC and Iñaki experimented together with this acoustic support.

A whispered masculine voice was recorded by the two microphones with this acoustic background. The voice appears to be a confirmation of Iñaki's comment that EVP voices (replies) sometimes occur before the operator asks the related question. Iñaki finished his talk with: (translation) "...this occurrence must logically mean that your time is distinct from the Earth chronological time".

The masculine voice says in Spanish *"Es distinto sí"* (It is distinct, yes). The inclusion appeared at minutes 8':17" of files 'U87 CONDENSER_DOL-PHINS' and 'SM57 DYNAMIC_DOLPHINS'. The files of the formal experiment were duly compared with the original music file and it was verified that the utterance does not exist in the original dolphins and music file.

The usual series of tests was performed but no other voices were detected.

4. Experiments in 2009

Operators

Professor Uwe Hartmann and his wife, Dr Ingrid Hartmann, came from Germany to take part in the tests. The Spanish operator Iñaki came from Toledo to participate again in the work.

Location of the tests

The sites were the same as previously indicated for the experiments in 2008.
A. EXPERIMENTS AT THE UNIVERSITY

Tests were carried out at Vigo University, Superior School of Engineering, at the Laboratory of Acoustics of the Dept. of Telecommunications, on July 23 from 15:00 to 19:00H. There was a new moon. Dr. Anabela Cardoso (AC), Dr. Ingrid Hartmann (IH), Prof. Uwe Hartmann (UH) participated as operators and Marco Lima (ML) as Sound Technician. During the experiments AC, IH and UH stayed in the recording room, whereas ML was in the technical room making the recordings (see the sketch below). This time the equipment did not belong to the University.

Three microphones were used:

Sennheiser MD 441 hyper cardioid, used with a preamplifier (property of UH). AKG C414 XLII in cardioid pattern (property of ML).

Groove Tubes GT57 in figure eight pattern (property of ML).

They were connected through the heavily mounted wall between the two rooms with the mixer (Xenyx802 8-input 2-bus Mic Preamp) and ML's recording computer in the technical room.

In parallel to the EVP experiments, measurements of the electrical and magnetic fields were continuously carried out. For this purpose a field meter:

"3D H/E Fieldmeter ESM-100 by Maschek, Germany, frequency area of the measurement: 5 Hz ... 400 kHz, 2 values per second" was used. The field meter was connected to a laptop in a little chamber beside the acoustic laboratory because of the heavy noise made by its hard disc.

A further computer (AC's laptop) was used in the laboratory to produce an explicit noise for the recordings[17] (See diagram).

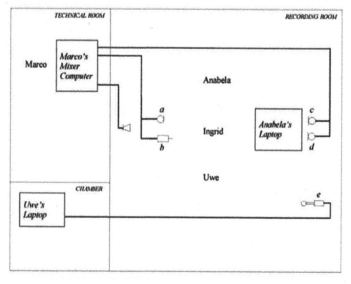

---

[17] The psychophon mentioned in b) of the diagram was not used because it malfunctioned.

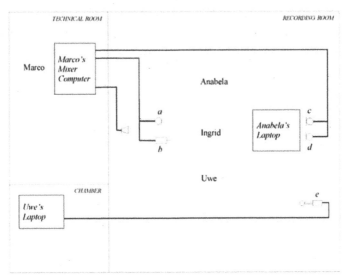

a - Sennheiser MD 441 with preamplifier
b - psychophon
c - AKG C414
d - Groove Tubes GT 57
e - Fieldmeter ESM-100

Two types of noise were used:

a) Frequency mixture - a file with pink noise was created by a computer in the technical room and sent over into the recording room where it was played by a loudspeaker.
b) Phoneme mixture – the aforementioned EVP-maker.

Two wave-files in Portuguese (a poem read by AC) and German (a text read by UH) were previously created as acoustic source for the EVP-maker program. The speech files were reversed with the software Sound Forge and at the Laboratory of Acoustics were fed into the EVP-maker software, which sliced them into small bits of words corresponding to approximately the length of syllables; the resulting EVP-maker noise was directly played back live on a computer in the recording room through the computer loudspeaker.

Procedure

Firstly, the background noise of the room without additional noise sources and in the absence of the experimenters was recorded, followed by a recording of background noise with additional pink noise. This recording also took place in the room without the experimenters. In a third experiment, the background noise with additional pink noise in the presence of two experimenters (IH and UH who remained silent in the room) was recorded.

After these preliminary measurements two recordings were carried out. Operators AC, IH and UH were in the recording room: Recordings of a conversation between the operators with additional pink noise. Talk and questions in English and German (duration: 8 min 52 sec). Recordings of a conversation between the operators with additional EVP-maker noise. Initially the EVP-maker noise based on the Portuguese language was used; secondly, the EVP-maker noise based on the German language was used. Talk and questions in English and German (duration: 12 min). During all recordings the E/M field was measured continuously with the Fieldmeter in 3 dimensions. The Fieldmeter produced a data set per 0, 5 sec storing it in a file.

Recordings Previous to the Experiments

Extra voices, apparently anomalous, appeared recorded on the computer hard disk during the initial period of preparation for the experiments while testing the cable connections, the position of the microphones, recording levels, etc. These recordings were never meant to be an informal experiment such as the one above mentioned with AC and Iñaki chatting in the corridor of the Laboratory of Acoustics. They were done purely for technical reasons.

At minute 01':33, 6" a full sentence in Portuguese appeared recorded, seeming to have replaced AC's talk in English with UH. The feminine voice is very different from AC's voice and says with singing intonation: "*Estamos aqui nós todos!*" at -44,3dB ("We are here all of us!"). It is clearer in the Sennheiser MD 441 hyper cardioid used with a preamplifier (File 441_01) and in the Groove Tubes GT57 in figure eight pattern recordings but practically inaudible in the AKG C414 XLII in cardioid pattern. At 1':39,5" again a feminine voice says in Portuguese: "*Nós estamos aqui, vamos ter respei [to]*" (We are here we'll be respect [ful]) with an amplitude peak of -44,7 dB. Similarly it seems to have replaced AC's voice talking in English to UH who does not understand a word of Portuguese. The amplitude of both sentences, and of the whole recording, is very low but, when amplified, both become perfectly clear and understandable to any listener proficient in Portuguese. The equipment was being tested and preliminary arrangements for the experiments were being carried out. The experimenters' voices talking to each other reach a peak of only around -36db in the Sennheiser MD 441 recording and the environmental noise is around -45dB, while the environmental noise is inferior to -66dB in the AKG C414 recording and to -63dB in the Groove Tubes GT57.

Voices Recorded During the Preparation for the Recordings With Additional Pink Noise

Similar acoustic events happened during the preparation for recording tests with additional pink noise. A couple of feminine voices seem to speak coherently in Portuguese. Nevertheless, the situation is confusing because the operators were in the chamber preparing the equipment and chatting, sometimes all at the same time. It seems risky to avow the paranormality of these voices because, in addition, the recording levels were set far too low and that adds to the muddle. These voices and the utterances above mentioned, although clear when amplified and easily understandable by any native of the language, will not be considered for the purposes of the present investigation. They are too low and muddled with the experimenters' conversations. Reference is made to them to illustrate the ambiguity and uncertainty of judgement created by unclear and disordered speech, notwithstanding the fact that the voices may be anomalous and their formation probably favoured by the same conditions that compel this author to discard them, i.e., a state of acoustic disorder.

However, during the preparation for one of the experiments, before the pink noise was played in the chamber, an unexpected voice was recorded by the different means, which should be considered in the scope of this report. AC engaged in conversation with IH while UH did the technical arrangements for a new experiment. When AC suddenly asked IH about Ernst Senkowski's health, IH hesitated uttering "Ahn, Ahn, yeah, yeah" in an attempt to find the appropriate English words to reply. At this point (01':35" of 'file 441_13' or '414_12'), a masculine voice can be heard in the recording saying simultaneously with

Ingrid's interjections and as if coming from behind her voice: "*Geisler!*". It has an amplitude peak of -31db (file '441_13') while the operators' voices vary between -25db and - 34db in the same file. The formal experiment started at 02':11" of the same file.

AC's limited knowledge of German did not allow her to decide about the meaning of "*Geisler*", quite an unusual word. According to the dictionary, it can mean different things as found out by UH who was also puzzled by it: "spartan man / ascetic / fakir/ hostage/ brotherhood whose members used to flagellate themselves singing the "Geißlerlieder" in the 13th-14th century/ slaughterer of little animals". In view of this, it was decided to ask Professor Ernst Senkowski if he had a hint of what this word, interposed in a conversation about him, could mean. Quote from his reply to this author:

De: Dr. Ernst Senkowski
[mailto:ernst.senkowski@t-online.de]
Enviado el: martes, 21 de diciembre de 2010 12:28
Para: Anabela Cardoso

Asunto: Re: interview
Dear -a-
....
The case GEISLER is a wonderful 100% transpersonal hit!
1 .GERT GEISLER was a long time chief editor of the magazine ESOTERA in Freiburg. I am not sure whether I was once in personal contact with him. But DETERMEYER must have been because he published at least two articles on ITC [EVP] in that journal, in 1979 and 1980.
2. Remarkably the name GEISLER manifested when you spoke about SENKOWSKI.
3.Senkowski's just now answering your interview questions about the HARSCH [Harsch-Fischbach couple] and asked himself whether he should implement the case of the computer graphic that appeared in black and white in Luxembourg, Dec. 4, 1988 for 70 sec. After the Harsch had somehow published it, DELAVRE found it more or less by chance in June 1989 as a coloured picture in ESOTERA, 3/1987...

An exceptional synchronicity seems to have manifested in this case. Neither AC nor the German operators perceived this intruding voice during their careful listening in 2009 to the materials recorded in the experiments, either together or separately. AC heard it for the first time when she communicated the fact to UH and IH and to Professor Senkowski that is, around the 18th of December 2010, while simultaneously working on the present report and on an interview with Dr. Senkowski about events that prominently included the case of an anomalous image received by experimenters Maggy and Jules Harsch-Fischbach, very similar to the image published by the magazine *Esotera* (Cardoso 2010), of which Gert Geisler was the chief editor. Ernst Senkowski was also working on the questions he had received from AC and thinking about that specific case, at the precise moment he received AC's E-mail asking about *"Geisler"*. To this date, and despite the many enquiries realised, it was not possible to find the whereabouts of Gert Geisler or if he is deceased or alive.

Experiment with Human Phonemes as Background Acoustic Support

In the formal experiments with the EVP-maker as source of explicit noise, no additional voices could be detected. However, some clear voices appeared recorded on the computer hard disc during the test recordings done before the start of the EVP-maker formal experiments.

One of the most interesting ones was the word *"Uwe"* (the forename of one experimenter) recorded at 01':31" in the files indicated below. Although very low in amplitude (-45dB), it is thoroughly clear. It occurred during a pause in the conversation between UH and AC, when no additional background noise of any kind was being played. Uwe and Anabela were discussing the setting up and testing the equipment. The EVP-maker software was not yet playing. Before the voice, two very low metallic clicks of undetermined origin occurred in the recording. No other sound can be heard in the recording when this voice was registered and therefore, in spite of its low amplitude, the word *"Uwe"* (with accent in the last syllable) is clearly audible and understandable to anybody with normal hearing ability. The utterance has the intonation typical of an old lady's voice. UH and IH thought it was reminiscent of UH's deceased grandmother's voice. The recording was saved purely by chance because it occurred without any experiment.

The next apparently anomalous voice recorded was the Portuguese sentence *"Há record"* (There is record). The English word "record" is pronounced with a typical Portuguese accent (recór). It happened one second after UH started the EVP-maker babble at 02':21" and it is preceded by two loud clicks which could have been produced by the computer mouse. Again, it is of interest that the apparently anomalous voice comes immediately after the clicks (independently of their nature). The occurrence of clicks and metallic noises, some of undetermined origin, immediately preceding the appearance of the supposed anomalous voices, happened in many of the experiments carried out in the scope of the present research project. The feminine voice is different from AC's reversed voice used by the EVP-maker software and it seems to have a different spatial positioning; it can be heard in the background of AC's reversed and chopped talk. Although clearly audible and understandable, it is softer than the babble. It is pertinent to the situation since the formal recording was going to start.

Another apparently anomalous voice, clear, loud and highly pertinent to the context says *"Certamente assim"* ("Certainly so"). The voice can be heard at 04':13" when AC finishes a brief talk with IH about the inconvenience of the EVP-maker software, saying: "...it is very easy to understand things there [in the EVP-maker babble] which are not there", meaning, naturally, pareidolia. The fact that the youngish, feminine voice has a Brazilian accent and its content corroborates AC's statement about the inappropriateness of the EVP-maker for serious tests is understandably a factor of great importance when pondering the anomalous nature of this sentence.

Other inclusions, also possibly anomalous, were found during playback. One of those, at 03':17", sounded like *"Sprachen!"* (German: "talked" or "spoke"); it appeared immediately after AC asked "What do we do?" The EVP-maker program had been fed with a reversed file in Portuguese and the word sounds like German. Another inclusion, albeit less clear, was found when the experiment finished and UH told the sound technician loudly "Stop it! [the recording]". A masculine voice, apparently different from UH's, which had been used in the EVP-maker babble, can be heard in the recordings saying *"they stop it"* (at 11':56, 58").

No extra voices were detected in the formal experiment, which used the EVP-maker babble as acoustic support and only started at 04': 37".

With the exception of the word *"Uwe"*, formed when there was no other noise, the important question in regard to the other voices abovementioned is whether these are indeed anomalous inclusions or, on the other hand, combinations of phonemes randomly arranged by the EVP-maker software, which happen to be relevant to the question/situation. It is extremely difficult to know for sure because of the high degree of uncertainty introduced by this method; the voices are included in the report because of their pertinence to the context and, mainly, the Brazilian accent of one of them, but they should be viewed from this perspective. All three feminine voices, presumably anomalous - *Há record"*, *"Certamente assim"* and *"Sprachen!"* - sound different from each other. The voices can be heard in all three recordings - Files 441_14, 414_13 and fig 8_14, albeit at different amplitudes.

As previously emphasized in regard to the other experiments, a remarkable feature of the unexplained voices recorded at the Acoustics Laboratory before the start of the formal experiments, is that they occurred in a somewhat confused recording situation involuntarily created by sound technician ML. He did not know the Laboratory of Acoustics and had to set up, adjust and test the equipment several times. Testing and several preliminary recordings done with different sophisticated microphones lasted for a couple of hours.

Measurements

During the occurrence of the voices, no changes of the measured E/M fields were detectable. The measured E/M field was constant in all measured dimensions during all recordings in the ranges:

Ex 1,3 .. 2,0 V/m, Ey 19,6 .. 20,7 V/m, Ez 25,0 .. 29,2 V/m

Hx 8 .. 9 nT, Hy 7 .. 8 nT, Hz 7 .. 8 nT

During the measurements the temperature was constant, 23° C (because of the air-conditioning); the humidity was 56% and the air pressure 957 hpa.

B. EXPERIMENTS AT THE METROPOLIS

Another set of experiments was carried out at the Metropolis in Vigo on 6.07.2009 from 21.00H to 23.30H. The moon was waxing. Participants were Dr. Anabela Cardoso, Dr. Ingrid Hartmann, Prof. Uwe Hartmann, José Ignacio Carmona (Iñaki) and Sound Technician Alfonso Garcia Agulla (Esky).

Room and Equipment of the Experiment

During the experiments AC, IH, UH and Iñaki were in the recording room whereas Esky and two technicians of the studio were in the technical room managing the recording (see sketch below).[18] There was visual contact between the operators and the technicians through the double-glass window for giving instructions. The following devices were used:

Sennheiser MD 441 hyper cardioids microphone (used without the preamplifier), property of UH.

Neumann U87 condenser microphone in omni-directional mode, property of Metropolis.

Shure SM58 dynamic microphone, property of Metropolis.

The Mac Computer of the Metropolis equipped with the ProTools professional software was connected to a Mixer in the technical room.

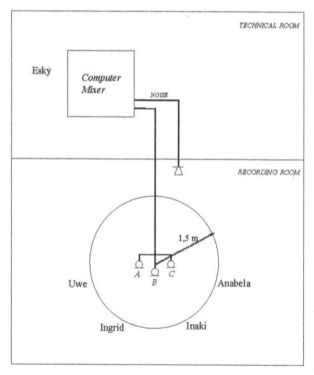

---

[18] The sketch displays the Metropolis technical facilities. Only the devices, the number and identities of the operators varied throughout the experiments.

A - Sennheiser MD441
B - Neumann U87
C - Shure SM58

Noise Source

The additional pink noise was created directly on the Mac computer of the studio and transmitted online from the technical room to a loudspeaker in the recording room. Pink noise instead of white noise was taken because of the softer sound.

Procedure

The temperature was 20°C (constant because of the air-conditioning). Two recordings were carried out:
- a recording of the conversation between AC, IH, UH and Iñaki without any additional noise (duration: 20 min 30 sec).
- a recording of talk and questions by AC, IH, UH and Iñaki with additional pink noise.

In the second test, the operators were particularly attentive to using clear, loud and emphasized speech. Unnecessary sounds were avoided during all the recordings. Speech and breaks were clearly separated. The operators' talk (a short speech) was followed by a long pause. A relaxed atmosphere prevailed.

Results

The first experiment consisted of an informal conversation between the operators without explicit background noise. An apparently anomalous voice was recorded. A soft feminine voice, very melodious and beautiful, utters what is easily perceived as *"altus"*. This is clearly audible but no meaning or context could be found for *"altus"*. However, since the voice seems to have a foreign accent, could this be the beginning of *"altered state"*? Furthermore, the voice seems to continue softly but it is 'buried' under AC's loud comment that immediately follows. The voice appeared recorded in the context of a conversation about altered states of consciousness, after Iñaki described in Spanish (he does not speak English) his usual EVP experimentation, affirming that he gets better results late at night, when he is extremely tired and falls into a kind of semi-altered state of consciousness. AC was ready to translate for the Hartmanns but made a pause and said a couple of words in Spanish before proceeding to the English. The voice appeared recorded between AC's words in Spanish and the continuation in English, while UH asked for the translation. The meaning of this voice must remain open.

The voice has a peak of around half the amplitude of the experimenter's voice. It is loudest in the U87 condenser microphone recording (the amplitude of the operator's voice is -14dB and the anomalous voice is -25, 5 dB in the U87 recording). (Files U-87_01, md 441_01 and sm 58_01 at 19′:13″).

No voices were detected in the experiment consisting of questions with additional pink noise.

Uncontrolled experiment held at an idyllic site by the brook "Além" near the town of Mondariz in Galicia, Spain on July 25.

An informal experiment was carried out during an excursion to the location above mentioned. The day was hot and the three operators, AC, IH and UH, sat beside a beautiful creek, chatted and asked questions to the communicators in a pleasant and tranquil atmosphere. The soft sound of running water was used as acoustic background. The atmosphere was friendly and relaxed. The moon was waxing. No proper extra voices were recorded. A couple of whispers can be perceived but those have not been considered in the scope of the present investigation because their low amplitude and mingling with the water sounds prevent any reliable interpretation and classification since pareidolia could easily occur. Mention is made of this experiment with the purpose of comparing the operators' psychological state of mind with the one prevailing during the other experiments and preceding arrangements when tension and tiredness were certainly greater.

Conclusions

The reality of the apparently anomalous electronic voices was confirmed in acoustically controlled environments with different operators.

With the exception of the June 17, 2008 radio voices, none of the voices or whispers described in the present report were heard live during the tests. Extra voices, originating from undetectable sources, were identified in the following situations:

1. Under controlled speech and controlled acoustic environment – AC as sole operator at the Metropolis and at the University of Vigo; Iñaki at the University of Vigo and at the Metropolis.

2. Under controlled acoustic environment and uncontrolled speech - AC, Portuguese operators and participants (PN and Francisco) at the Metropolis; AC, IH and UH at University of Vigo; the same and Iñaki at the Metropolis.

3. Under uncontrolled speech and uncontrolled acoustic environment - AC and the Portuguese operators outside the Acoustics chamber of the Superior School of Engineering; AC and Iñaki at the same place. The voices seemed to benefit from the presence of noise in the environment (particularly human speech and metallic clicks). The very few voices recorded without any explicit noise had quite lower amplitude than the voices registered with a background of explicit noise. The amplitude of the voices seems to be related to the level of background environmental noise extant in the room when the voices appear recorded. Probably to other variables, too but those remain undefined and need further research.

The voices were louder, clearer, more abundant and flowing when uncontrolled direct human speech by two or more people prevailed, independently of an acoustically controlled or uncontrolled environment.

Above all, they seemed to benefit from a situation where the operators' frame of mind was lively and energetic, and perhaps also from a relaxed and friendly atmosphere. On the other hand, they seemed to be negatively affected if the operators were focused on the experiment.

The voices seemed to benefit from a slightly chaotic situation - AC, Portuguese operators, PN and Francisco at the Metropolis; AC, IH, UH and Sound Technician ML at the Laboratory of Acoustics.

The voices did not seem to be significantly more abundant when an artificial basis of human speech was used (Psychophone and EVP-maker) as acoustic background source. Both methods, the Psychophone and the EVPmaker software, proved to be highly unreliable not because they are particularly bad acoustic backgrounds for the production of the voices but because they are undoubtedly a source of uncertainty and ambiguity in the analysis of the results. They can very easily originate pareidolia and/or projection of meaning based upon expectation. Very particularly with the EVP-maker software, it is easy to find 'results' in recording-sessions where they do not exist. In addition, an erroneous interpretation of the content of possibly anomalous utterances found in the recording is very likely. Most of the EVP 'results', published in the Internet, fall into one of these categories.

The equipment and location of the experiments did not seem to weigh on the formation of the voices but the highly sensitive microphone Bruel & Kjaer used at some of the University experiments appeared to capture more voices than the other microphones.

The content of all the voices recorded in the tests, with the possible exception of *"altus"*, were pertinent to the situation and/or to the operator/s.

From the results of the present research, this author fully corroborates Professor Alex Schneider, the Swiss physicist from St. Gallen who closely followed, studied and replicated some of Raudive's work, when he declares in his Appendix to *Breakthrough*:

"Other investigators choose the moment when a transmitter starts to beam out the carrier wave just before beginning to transmit a programme or else they select a slow-speaking lecture programme in which the pauses between groups of words are so considerable that call signs can be interspersed. A carrier appears to be necessary, or, at any rate, desirable ... a number of voices sound as though they were constituted from the homogeneous noise spectrum by some physically unexplained process of selection" (ibid, pp.340-341).

Moreover, in view of the results, a pertinent question is to find out if there are parallels between the allegedly anomalous electronic voice phenomena and so-called paranormal events of a different nature. Apparently, one of the distinctive characteristics of paranormal events is their occurrence in situations when they cannot easily be controlled. Prof. Hans Bender is quoted as saying (translation):

"If we tentatively admit the still questionable factuality of 'spooks', then [the attempt] to keep hold of it by photographing, filming or by recording acoustical phenomena will have to face the difficulty that the phenomena apparently elude a critical grasp. The impression almost suggests that the intelligent forces mock the observer and produce a phenomenon just there where one cannot get hold of it" (Bender, 1979).

Recorded Voices

Date/Place	Operators	Execution	Additional	Voices (translation)	Loudness	Intelligibility	Semantic Reference
17.06.2008 Metropolis	AC	controlled environment controlled speech	Sony radio hiss	"Está no estúdio" (["He] is in the studio")	sufficient	sufficient	yes (reply to AC's question if Konstantin Raudive could hear her)
				"falamos p' ra ..." ("We speak for...")	deficient	deficient	
27.06.2008 Metropolis	AC PN	controlled environment controlled speech		"Somos nós (Luis)" ("It is us (Luis)")	good	good	yes (confirmation of communicators' identity when AC addressed Rio do Tempo)
26.07.2008 Metropolis	AC, Luísa, Maria Anjos, PN, Francisco	controlled environment, uncontrolled speech	No: animated conversation between operators/participants	"e um pouco envergonhado" ("and a little ashamed [timid]") "já estou a ficar nervosa" ("I am already getting nervous") "this is hot!"	Very good	excellent	yes (possible anticipated comments about a dialogue between AC and PN that followed)
(no experiment)		controlled environment controlled speech	Reversed operators' and participants' voices used as acoustic background	"Felipe", "Felipe da Silva"	good	good	yes (reply to operator Maria Anjos' question)

Date/Place Operators	Execution	Additional noise	Voices (translation)	Rating Loudness	Rating Intelligibility	Semantic Reference
28.07.2008 U. Vigo AC, Luisa, Maria Anjos, PN,	controlled environment controlled speech	University CD with white noise	"Está aqui o Cardoso". ("Cardoso is here")	sufficient	good	yes (reply to AC's question if the communicators were in the Lab)
Francisco	uncontrolled environment uncontrolled speech	No added noise but a screeching sound, possibly	"Estamos aqui por cima" ("We are here above")	Good	Very good	Not directly (it can be interpreted as explanation of the communicators' situation in regard to the
		made by the door, can be heard in the recording	"Só isso!" ("Only that! [That's all]")	sufficient	good	yes (the recording had just started)
06.08.2008 U. Vigo AC, Iñaki, PN	controlled environment, controlled speech	no	"Somos capazes sim" ("We are able, yes")	poor	poor	yes (reply to Iñaki's question if the communicators were able to read his thought)
			Dog barks	Very good	excellent	yes (anticipated reply to Iñaki's request to his deceased dog for a sign)

Date/Place Operators	Execution	Additional noise	Voices (translation)	Rating Loudness	Intelligibility	Semantic Reference
06.08.2008 U. Vigo AC, Iñaki, PN	Uncontrolled environment, uncontrolled speech (informal experiment)	No; operators chatted casually and animatedly	"Ment[i]es paseo yo en Vigo!" ("In the meantime I'll wander through Vigo!")	very good	good	possible (it could be related to the context)
			"Há passagem" ("There is passage")	sufficient	sufficient	possible (it could be related to the context)
	controlled environment, controlled speech		"Per[o] huye" ("But [he] runs away") "No cree!" ("[He] does not believe!")	good	very good	possible (it could be related to the context
	controlled environment, controlled speech	no	"Era o contacto" ("It was the contact...")	Very deficient	deficient	yes (reply to Iñaki's request to the communicators to testify that the contact is feasible)
07.08.2008 Metropolis AC, Inaki	controlled environment, controlled speech	Audio file of music mixed with dolphin shrieks and water sounds	"Es distinto sí" ("It is distinct, yes")	deficient	deficient	yes (reply to Iñaki's comment that the communicators' time is distinct from Earth time)
13.11.2008 Metropolis AC	controlled environment, controlled speech	No: 3 micros; psychophone: 1 micro	"Contacto pode fazer no rádio" ("Contact you can make in [through] the radio"	deficient	deficient	yes (reply to AC's question if the psycho-phone was a good method for EVP)

Date/Place	Execution	Additional	Voices		Rating		Semantic Reference
Operators		noise		(translation)	Loudness	Intelligibility	
23.07.2009 U. Vigo	controlled environment uncontrolled speech	No	"Geisler"		*good*	good	remote
AC, IH, UH ML			"Uwe"		poor	excellent	yes (name of one operator present)
	controlled environment no speech	reversed EVP-maker output of a Portuguese poem	"Há record" ("There is record")		good	good	yes (the recording had just started)
	controlled environment, uncontrolled speech	reversed EVP-maker output of a Portuguese poem	"Certamente assim" ("Certainly so")		good	Very good	yes (reply to Anabela's comment about the inconveniences of the EVP-maker))
			"sprachen!" ("talked!" or "spoke!")		good	good	yes (possible comment about Anabela's question: "What do we do?"
			"they stop it"		sufficient	sufficient	yes (possible comment about Uwe's request: Please stop it!")
26.07.2009 Metropolis AC, IH, UH, Iñaki, Esky	controlled environment, uncontrolled speech	no	"altus"		sufficient	sufficient	no

References

Bander P. *Carry on Talking, How Dead Are the Voices?* Gerrards Cross, UK: Colin Smythe. Ltd. 1972.

Bander P. *Voices from the Tapes.* New York: Drake Publishers Inc, 1973.

Bayless R. "Electronic communication". *Journal of the Academy of Religion and Psychical Research* 1980; 3(1): 37-40.

Bender H. Zur Analyse aussergewöhnlicher Stimmphänomene auf Tonband. Erkundungsexperimente über dir « Einspielungen » von Friedrich Jürgenson. ZSPP (Zeitschrift für Parapsychologie und Grenzgebiete der Psychologie), 12, N 4, 226-238, Freiburg i. Br: Walter-Verlag, 1970.

Bender H. The Phenomena of Friedrich Jürgenson. *Journal of Paraphysics*, 1972;6 (2):65-75.

Bender H. Verborgene Wirklichkeit. Munich: Deutscher Taschenbuch Verlag, 1976.

Bender H. Die Gleichförmigkeit von "Spuk"-Mustern in: Zeitschrift für Parapsychologie und Grenzgebiete der Psychologie 1979; 21: 133-139.

Bender H. On the Analysis of Exceptional Voice Phenomena on Tapes. Pilot studies on the 'recordings' of Friedrich Jürgenson. ITC Journal 2011; 40: 61-78.

Cardoso A. Brief remarks on ITC: EVP experimentation. *ITC Journal* 2001; 8: 12-16.

Cardoso A. *Electronic Voices: Contact with Another Dimension?* Ropley, Hants, UK: O Books - John Hunt Publishing, Ltd, 2010.

Cardoso A. CD: Electronic Voices (available from www.itcjournal.org), 2010.

Cardoso A. Ernst Senkowski talks with Anabela Cardoso. *ITC Journal* 2010; 39: 35-60.

Carmona J. Psicofonias: El enigma de la Transcomunicación Instrumental. Madrid: Ediciones Nowtilus S. L, 2010.

Jürgenson F. *Röstema från Rymden* (Voices from the Space). Stockholm: Saxon & Lindströms, 1964.

Jürgenson F. Sprechfunk mit Verst*orbenen* (Freiburg im Br.: Verlag Hermann Bauer. Republished 1981 by Goldmann Verlag (München), 1967.

Jürgenson F. Radio och Mikrofonkontakt med de döda. (Radio and microphone contacts with the dead). Uppsala: Nybloms, 1968.

Jürgenson F. *Voice Transmissions with the Deceased*. Stockholm: Firework Edition N° 101. The Jürgenson Foundation: http://www.fargfabriken.se/fjf/, 2004

Raudive K. Unhörbares Wird Hörbar – Auf den Spuren Einer Geisterwelt. Remagen: Reichl, 1968.

Raudive K. *Breakthrough: An Amazing Experiment in Electronic Communication with the Dead*. Gerrards Cross, England: Colin Smythe, 1971.

Scott Rogo D. and Bayless R. *Phone Calls from the Dead*. Englewood Cliffs, New Jersey: Prentice-Hall, 1979.

Senkowski E. Instrumentelle Transkommunikation (first ed.1989) Frankfurt: R. G. Fischer, 1995.

Paperbacks also available from
White Crow Books

Jesus of Nazareth with Simon Parke—
Conversations with Jesus of Nazareth
ISBN 978-1-907661-41-9

Thomas à Kempis with Simon
Parke—*The Imitation of Christ*
ISBN 978-1-907661-58-7

Julian of Norwich with Simon
Parke—*Revelations of Divine Love*
ISBN 978-1-907661-88-4

Allan Kardec—*The Spirits Book*
ISBN 978-1-907355-98-1

Allan Kardec—*The Book on Mediums*
ISBN 978-1-907661-75-4

Emanuel Swedenborg—*Heaven and Hell*
ISBN 978-1-907661-55-6

P.D. Ouspensky—*Tertium Organum:
The Third Canon of Thought*
ISBN 978-1-907661-47-1

Dwight Goddard—*A Buddhist Bible*
ISBN 978-1-907661-44-0

Michael Tymn—*The Afterlife Revealed*
ISBN 978-1-970661-90-7

Michael Tymn—*Transcending the
Titanic: Beyond Death's Door*
ISBN 978-1-908733-02-3

Guy L. Playfair—*If This Be Magic*
ISBN 978-1-907661-84-6

Guy L. Playfair—*The Flying Cow*
ISBN 978-1-907661-94-5

Guy L. Playfair —*This House is Haunted*
ISBN 978-1-907661-78-5

Carl Wickland, M.D.—
Thirty Years Among the Dead
ISBN 978-1-907661-72-3

John E. Mack—*Passport to the Cosmos*
ISBN 978-1-907661-81-5

Peter & Elizabeth Fenwick—
The Truth in the Light
ISBN 978-1-908733-08-5

Erlendur Haraldsson—
Modern Miracles
ISBN 978-1-908733-25-2

Erlendur Haraldsson—
At the Hour of Death
ISBN 978-1-908733-27-6

Erlendur Haraldsson—
The Departed Among the Living
ISBN 978-1-908733-29-0

Brian Inglis—*Science and Parascience*
ISBN 978-1-908733-18-4

Brian Inglis—*Natural and Supernatural:
A History of the Paranormal*
ISBN 978-1-908733-20-7

Ernest Holmes—*The Science of Mind*
ISBN 978-1-908733-10-8

Victor & Wendy Zammit —*A Lawyer
Presents the Evidence For the Afterlife*
ISBN 978-1-908733-22-1

Casper S. Yost—*Patience
Worth: A Psychic Mystery*
ISBN 978-1-908733-06-1

William Usborne Moore—
Glimpses of the Next State
ISBN 978-1-907661-01-3

William Usborne Moore—
The Voices
ISBN 978-1-908733-04-7

John W. White—
The Highest State of Consciousness
ISBN 978-1-908733-31-3

Stafford Betty—
The Imprisoned Splendor
ISBN 978-1-907661-98-3

Paul Pearsall, Ph.D. —
Super Joy
ISBN 978-1-908733-16-0

**All titles available as eBooks, and selected titles available in Hardback and
Audiobook formats from www.whitecrowbooks.com**

Printed in August 2023
by Rotomail Italia S.p.A., Vignate (MI) - Italy